Die Deutsche Bibliothek –
CIP-Cataloguing-in-Publication-Data
A catalogue record for this
publication is available from
Die Deutsche Bibliothek

Library of Congress
Cataloguing-in-Publication is available

©2001, Foster and Partners, London,
and Prestel Verlag, Munich, London,
New York

Prestel Verlag
Mandlstrasse 26
80802 Munich
Germany
Tel +49 (089) 381709-0
Fax +49 (089) 381709-35
sales@prestel.de

175 Fifth Ave.
Suite 402
New York NY 10010
USA
Tel +1 (212) 995-2720
Fax +1 (212) 995-2733
sales@prestel-usa.com

4 Bloomsbury Place
London WC1A 2QA
United Kingdom
Tel +44 (020) 7323-5004
Fax +44 (020) 7636-8004
sales@prestel-uk.co.uk

Printed in Spain
ISBN 3-7913-2541-8
D.L.: M-25602-2001

Norman Foster
and The British Museum

Norman Foster
Deyan Sudjic
Spencer de Grey

Prestel Munich · London · New York

Contents

Preface	6
Rediscovering the Great Court	14
A Project Diary	38
Elements of the Great Court	68
Facts and Figures	112
Team Credits	116
Further Reading	119
Credits	120

Preface
Norman Foster

The courtyard at the heart of the British Museum was one of London's long-lost spaces. In the middle of the nineteenth century, for a brief few years, there was a garden in the middle of the Museum. This was soon occupied by the magnificent drum of the round Reading Room and what remained of the courtyard was filled in with an ad hoc collection of bookstacks. Without this space the Museum lacked a central focus – it was like a city without a park. Our project is about its reinvention.

In terms of its number of visitors – approaching six million a year – the British Museum is more popular than the Louvre in Paris or the Metropolitan Museum in New York. That degree of popularity puts severe demands on the building. Over the years it caused a critical level of congestion throughout the Museum: before the advent of the Great Court visitors struggled through one gallery in order to get to the next one. The departure of the British Library from the site presented the opportunity to address these problems and to regenerate the Museum for future centuries.

One of our earliest drawings explored the way in which the Great Court lies along a new heritage route that runs through London like a ley line from the British Library in the north, to Covent Garden and the South Bank. We saw that we could create a new public route through the building and, in doing so, achieve a better balance between the Museum as an entity and the city as a larger whole.

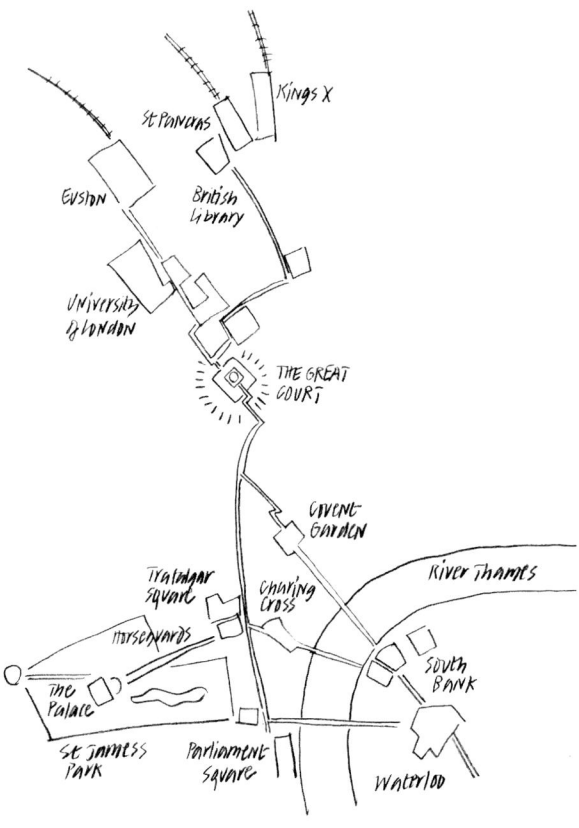

It followed that the Great Court should offer an urban experience in microcosm. Unlike other museums, where the first thing you see is the gift shop, as you enter the Great Court from the south, the drum of the Reading Room sits before you in the courtyard like a rotunda in a Renaissance città ideale, surrounded by the hustle and bustle of the Museum. In front of the Reading Room, Anish Kapoor's new sculpture will stand like an obelisk, marking the library entrance.

Just as in a historical European city you might move from a confined passageway into the grandeur of a formal piazza flooded with light, within the Great Court there are compressions and explosions of space. The varying profile of the new additions around the Reading Room drum has generated moments where you are almost within touching distance of a carved capital or the framing of the roof. At other points the space soars above you.

Again like a city, this variety of experiences encourages exploration. And it seems to work: the cafés are always crowded and sales in the bookshop have increased. This in turn has commercial benefits for the Museum.

Looking at a building on this scale – one that has grown and evolved over a period of 150 years – it is like a city in another sense, its fabric the product of different periods and styles. Along with the Royal Academy of Arts in London and the Reichstag in Berlin, the British Museum is one of a family of historical buildings in which we have made contemporary architectural interventions. In each case the new reveals something fresh about the old. At the Royal Academy we can enjoy the dialogue between Burlington's Palladian villa and the Victorian galleries across the inhabited lightwell between them. In the Reichstag we see history literally revealed – the Soviet graffiti, masons' marks and the scars of war.

When we first visited the British Museum the remnants of the Museum's courtyard were visible only from above; in fact few knew the courtyard existed at all. We have peeled back the layers of history to open it up once again as the heart of the building. The Great Court is both a new organisational hub and the catalyst for the Museum's reinvigoration. And the once virtually secret world of the Reading Room is now available to all.

Opposite: Drawing by Norman Foster showing how the Great Court forms both the heart of the Museum and a new urban short-cut, mediating between Bloomsbury and the new British Library in the north and Covent Garden and the Thames to the south.

Below left: Exterior view of the Reichstag in Berlin; its new glass cupola forms a contemporary counterpoint to the historical building and is animated by the movement of people on the ramps within.

Below right: View of the Carré d'Art in Nîmes; the new building has been the catalyst for social and economic renewal in the city, generating a new café life in the square in front of the building and the surrounding streets.

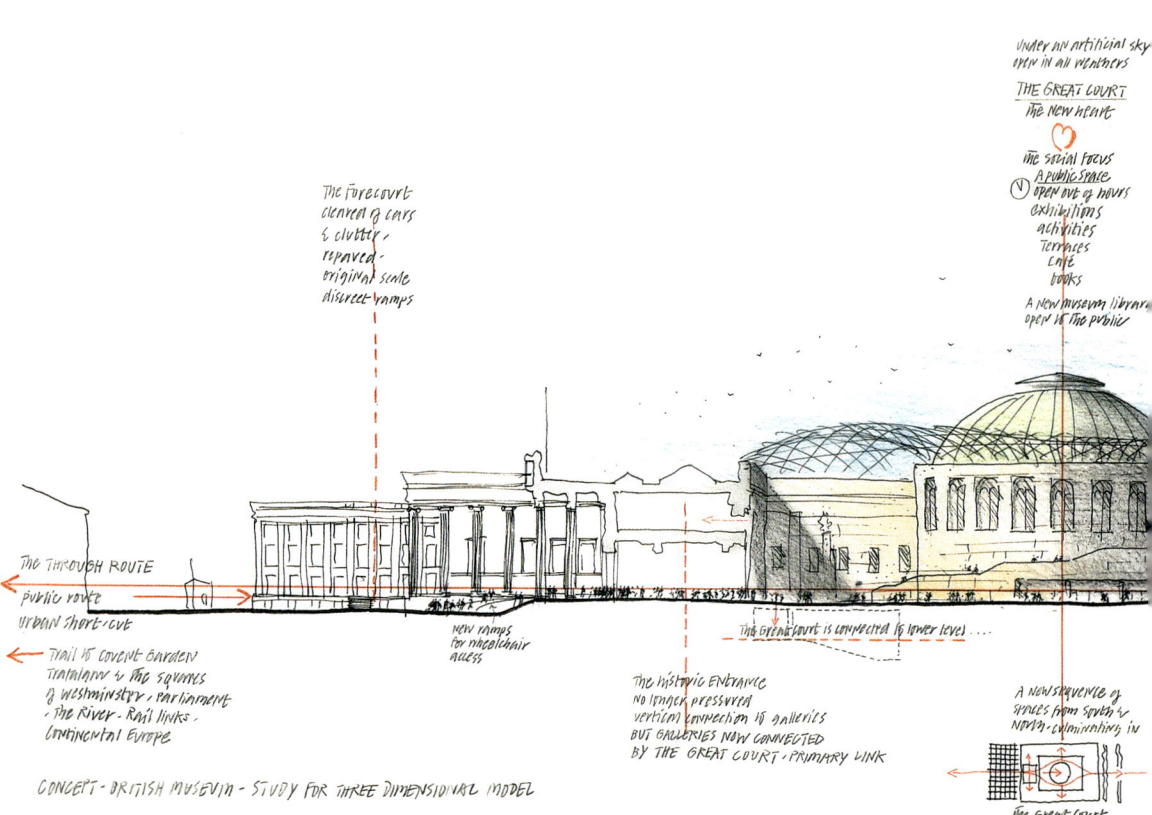

Norman Foster's drawing showing how the Great Court forms a new social and cultural plaza for the Museum and for London.

Above left: Buckminster Fuller's 1950 proposal for a dome over midtown Manhattan.

Above right: Interior view of the Crystal Palace of 1851, which pioneered the idea of a glass-roofed public gallery.

The glazed canopy that makes the activity of the Great Court possible fuses state-of-the-art engineering with economy of form. Its unique triangulated geometry results from the challenge of spanning the irregular gap between the dome of the Reading Room and the nineteenth-century courtyard facades, while its glazing maximises lightness and transparency and minimises solar gain. It is a unique form, which could not have been realised at any point in the Museum's past. But it too has a history.

Since our early collaborations with Buckminster Fuller on theoretical studies such as the Climatroffice – a free-form dome over a city site, within which buildings would have enjoyed their own microclimate – we have explored the potential of lightweight, transparent enclosures. Like Buckminster Fuller, we have always aimed to 'do the most with the least'.

One of the direct antecedents of the Great Court – our project for a transport interchange and office complex in Hammersmith – would have created the largest enclosed public space in Europe. Bigger than Trafalgar Square, sheltered beneath a translucent canopy and planted to evoke London's leafy garden squares, this urban room would have been 'green' in more than one sense: the enclosed volume formed a climatic buffer, which promised substantial energy savings for the adjacent buildings. The idea of a sheltering roof 'umbrella' can also be found in the undulating canopy of Stansted Airport, which allowed us to reinvent the airport, recasting the passenger concourse as a free-flowing, luminous space.

Although there is an echo in the Great Court of Buckminster Fuller's Manhattan dome, its urban roots lie elsewhere: in the exhibition halls, winter gardens and grand arcades of the nineteenth century and in some of our own projects of the recent past. Like the Galleria Vittorio Emanuele in Milan, for example – or the plaza created beneath our Commerzbank tower in Frankfurt – it is both a route through the Museum and a destination in its own right – a popular meeting point for those living and working in Bloomsbury.

The ability of a cultural amenity such as the Museum to provide the catalyst for social and economic renewal was powerfully demonstrated by our Carré d'Art in Nîmes, which has changed the fortunes of an entire city quarter. Of course, the outdoor café life that now thrives there reflects a benign southern climate. In the Great Court the glass sky creates a microclimate that similarly invites a leisurely approach to life. To promenade there, to buy a book or a magazine and read it over a coffee, is to enjoy an experience unlike that to be found anywhere else in London.

The Great Court can also be understood in the context of our 'World Squares for All' masterplan, which makes detailed proposals for the environmental improvement of Trafalgar Square, Parliament Square, Whitehall and their environs in central London. The scheme's emphasis is on improving pedestrian access and enhancing the settings of the area's many historical buildings and monuments – just as the newly restored forecourt in Bloomsbury adds to the dignity of the Museum and heralds the Great Court.

One of Buckminster Fuller's ambitions for his Manhattan dome was that it should promote fresh means of experiencing the city. Beneath its own glass sky the Great Court has created new ways of accessing and enjoying the Museum's collections and has pioneered patterns of social use hitherto unknown within this or any other museum. The Great Court is a new kind of civic space – a cultural plaza – which people are invited to use and enjoy from early in the morning to late at night. In a crowded city and a busy Museum it is an oasis.

Above: 'View of an Ideal City', circa 1470, attributed to Piero della Francesca.

Below: A design sketch by Norman Foster exploring how the new accommodation in the Great Court wraps around the Reading Room drum.

Rediscovering the Great Court
Deyan Sudjic

The Great Court at the British Museum is the product of the work of no less than three architects, along with a nineteenth-century librarian and the Museum's last twentieth-century director. Only the first of them, Sir Robert Smirke, who defined its shape and proportions, had an entirely free hand. And even he had to create a plan that allowed the Museum to be built in gradual stages around Montagu House, its original home, which in turn was demolished equally slowly. At the heart of the Museum was a great courtyard that Smirke saw as a fitting consummation of the expectations aroused by the heroic scale of the Ionic entrance.

Sydney Smirke, egged on by Antonio Panizzi, the brilliant Italian exile who made the Museum's Library one of the greatest of its kind in the world, obliterated his elder brother's courtyard by filling it with the round Reading Room. What had been a two-acre open space on the scale of Hanover Square – albeit one to which the general public was denied access – turned into a great domed interior, reserved for scholars, with a squalid hinterland of makeshift sheds and utilitarian bookstacks, which lapped like flotsam at the edges of the Library and the courtyard that contained it.

The third architect is Norman Foster who has transformed the centre of the Museum for a second time – pulling off the difficult feat of reconciling his predecessors' visions one with the other, allowing both courtyard and Reading Room to coexist.

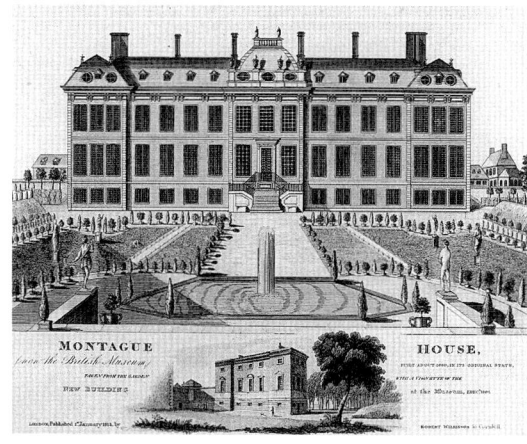

Opposite: An 1813 engraving of the garden facade of Montagu House, the first home of the British Museum.

Below: The south front of Robert Smirke's new Museum building, with its grand Ionic portico, as completed in 1848.

Above: An idealised mid-nineteenth-century view of the Museum's central courtyard, looking north. Although the courtyard was conceived by Smirke as an open garden, the public was never granted access to it.

Left: The Egyptian Sculpture Gallery, completed in the autumn of 1831, illustrated in a contemporary engraving.

In the run up to the Library's departure in 1998 to Colin St John Wilson's purpose-built home next to St Pancras Station, the Museum's director, Robert Anderson, began to think seriously about the implications of tearing such a hefty chunk out of the heart of the building. Until then, most of the strategic effort had been devoted to exploring ways of expanding the Museum on its existing site further into Bloomsbury. In the 1960s, Leslie Martin and Colin St John Wilson worked on a scheme that would have cleared a huge swathe of Georgian Bloomsbury, as far as Hawksmoor's church on High Holborn, carving out an open plaza with the Library on one side and creating a fine setting for the approach to the Museum. This did not go down well with the newly invented conservationist lobby, however. Wilson then drew up a more modest scheme to squeeze the Library into a reduced site that would still have required an unacceptable amount of demolition.

In 1994, for the first time, there was a realisation that the issue of what to do with the space released by the departure of the Library was likely to be just as problematic. To find a way to deal with the empty shell of the Library, and the mess that encircled it, Anderson and the Museum Trustees staged an architectural competition, which Foster and Partners won.

The Great Court is one of the most striking architectural experiences in London, without actually being a building in its own right. Foster has deftly drained the courtyard of debris to rediscover the ghost of the outdoor space that Robert Smirke intended. Like an archaeologist, Foster reveals what was once there, but cannot recreate the space lost by the installation of a giant Victorian cuckoo in a chaste Ionic nest. He allows both to coexist by turning negative into positive space, almost in the manner of one of Rachel Whiteread's cast concrete sculptures. The Great Court appears to take its character from its surroundings but it is anything but passive. It is an indoor space but only just. Under the extraordinary glass roof it is possible to watch the clouds glide by and to see the sun track across the stone floor.

The Great Court is more than a restoration. It is the creation of something powerfully, distinctively new. Certainly it is one of the most challenging commissions of Norman Foster's career and that of his partner, Spencer de Grey, who steered the project. It is also perhaps a defining one. It mixes architecture and urban design and it confronts the language of classicism with computer-generated structural design, providing a level of analysis never previously available. In this sense the roof over the courtyard has a shape that could not have existed at any other period.

Above: Visiting Orientalists studying the Rosetta Stone at the British Museum, from the Illustrated London News, September 1874.

The British Museum is the place where some of the greatest creations from many of the world's civilisations, from the Rosetta Stone to the Elgin Marbles, have ended up. From its Reading Room Leon Trotsky and Karl Marx set out to change the world. And it is also a complex organism with its own traditions, prejudices and inevitable conflicts.

This is far from Foster's first attempt to address a highly charged historical context. At the Royal Academy of Art's Sackler Galleries, there was also a play between classical context and steel and glass insertions, as well as the unlocking of a previously lost space. In Nîmes Foster worked alongside one of France's finest surviving Roman monuments to create the Carré d'Art; and in Berlin retaining the neo-Baroque shell of the Reichstag was a given, even though it was Foster's job to exorcise the ghosts of its troubled past.

Each of these projects provided clues for the Great Court but each of them was also the product of a rather different set of circumstances. In Berlin the raw evidence of the past – Soviet graffiti and vaults rudely deprived of their original mouldings – exists in sharp contrast to the new insertions. In the British Museum Foster and de Grey have chosen a different strategy. While the walls of the courtyard and the interiors of the Reading Room are allowed to speak for themselves, everything else is determinedly new and finished with extreme precision.

It is as if Foster is self-consciously expunging the humble, makeshift nature of the space as it was and dressing it to play the part of a national institution.

The Reading Room, encased in stone, girdled by sweeping twin staircases, stands at the centre of the Great Court as a monumental rotunda, connected only by the most tentative of glass links to Smirke's Museum to allow access from the existing upper-level galleries. Everything else is kept low-key. Access to the rest of Foster's work at the Museum – the lower-level lecture theatres, the locker rooms for school parties – is from a pair of stairs sunk into unobtrusive openings pressed against the south wall of the courtyard. To the north, in what will be the Wellcome Gallery, another pair of stairs lead to the new Sainsbury African Galleries.

As a visitor you are aware of the powerful presence of the stone-clad drum of the Reading Room even before you reach it. In the entrance hall that Smirke built, daylight now filters gently in, urging you on till you find yourself under that roof, with its fascinating, optically dynamic structure, in the authoritative presence of the round Reading Room with its frieze of inscribed lettering.

In its very nature, the British Museum has never been a static institution. Throughout the 250 years of its existence, it has continually changed shape and form, despite acquiring the thick crust of tradition that now gives the illusion of conservatism.

The Museum grew from several disparate private collections of natural curiosities, specimens, paintings, medals and books, to become the most significant repository of archaeological remains in the world, before metamorphosing once again to become one of the world's greatest libraries.

And yet at the same time the Museum has had within it the seeds of its eventual destruction. The more it has excelled at amassing a general collection, the greater has been the pressure for it to specialise. Continual expansion has inevitably led to subsequent eruptions. From being an attempt at a universal collection of everything, growth inevitably resulted in increasing specialisation. And most of those specialised collections have spun out of the original institution.

The Museum gave up its pictures to establish the National Gallery in 1828, a mere twelve years after acquiring its most famous exhibit, the Elgin Marbles. Its plant specimens, geological collections, birds and dinosaurs went to create the Natural History Museum in 1880. The space was filled by the massive expansion of the Museum's collections of books and documents. For a while it seemed that Panizzi, who created what eventually became the British Library, would swallow the Museum whole. 'Paris must be surpassed' he would urge his assistants, as the Museum overtook the Bibliothèque Nationale in size and importance, its collection of books and documents doubling and redoubling every ten years.

Finally, in 1998, after thirty years of plans and counterplans, the Library itself departed. That shift left a void at the very centre of the Museum, a space which Foster's Great Court fills paradoxically by not filling. Foster has created instead one of London's greatest new urban spaces. It offers a taste of what his vision of the new partially pedestrianised Trafalgar Square will be like.

The Museum has gone through a pattern of expansion and contraction that could almost be seen as a detailed working model of the 'Big Bang' theory of the creation of the universe, which the Museum might well display in one of its countless glass cabinets. In the beginning there was nothing. Nobody believed in building a free museum 'for the instruction and gratification of the public', as the Act of Parliament establishing the British Museum specified. Then suddenly and apparently without warning, floating clouds of dust fused to make the universe in a single creative explosion.

The Big Bang in this case is represented by the moment in 1753 when Parliament passed the Act accepting the bequest of a sprawling collection built up by Sir Hans Sloane, a highly successful physician and enthusiastic scientist.

Above left: A view of the Egyptian Sculpture Gallery shortly after the introduction of electric lighting, from the Illustrated London News, February 1890.

Above right: A print from the Illustrated London News of October 1850, announcing the arrival at the Museum of an Assyrian human-headed and winged lion sculpture from Nimrud.

Above: An engraving of the Reading Room, pictured shortly after its opening in May 1857.

Sloane had filled his house in Bloomsbury Place, and the one next door, with ever-growing numbers of exotic plants, fruits, corals, mineral stones, ferns, shells, fossils, coins, medals, classical and mediaeval antiquities and books. In 1742 he removed both himself and his collection to much larger premises in Chelsea. Sloane was an Enlightenment figure: Voltaire visited him, and when Handel came for tea, he outraged his host by thoughtlessly placing a buttered muffin on one of Sloane's rare manuscripts.

Sloane's collection was joined with that of Sir Robert Cotton, another avid collector who specialised in books and manuscripts, including the Lindisfarne Gospel, the Anglo-Saxon Chronicle and the Magna Carta. These private collections were acquired by the state and combined to make the core of the Museum. A lottery was authorised by Parliament to fund the housing of the collection, just as the National Lottery would later part-fund the Great Court.

Montagu House, a mansion built on the site of the present Museum in 1675, was acquired to house the collections, and so for the first 75 years of its existence, the British Museum showed its collections in the fundamentally domestic setting of a great house. While the Museum was open to the public free of charge, it was, in the early-nineteenth century, a very different place from its contemporary incarnation, with visitors numbered in thousands rather than millions.

There was very little artificial light and little attempt at explanation or display techniques. Visitors needed an admission ticket, which might take six months to acquire. Unless they were known to Museum staff, curious scholars and early tourists alike were marched around Montagu House by guides — one visitor described them as 'ciceroni' — who would rush them through as fast as possible, weaving past the cluster of stuffed giraffes on the main staircase, through the galleries of coins and books, until they were ushered back out into the street.

Even at this early stage it was clear that Europe's museums were already highly politicised institutions, used by governments as tools of foreign policy in the struggle for national supremacy. Louis XIV had been so eager to secure Cotton's manuscripts for France that he invited Cotton's grandson to name his price and offered a dukedom to sweeten the deal.

That rivalry is just as keen today, even if the Museum has grown from a primarily academic, scholarly institution into a vast social magnet, attracting almost six million visitors annually. Between them, the Louvre and the British Museum represent the commanding heights of the European museum world.

Below: The cast-iron framing of the Reading Room rising from the Museum's courtyard, shown in the Illustrated London News, April 1855.

During his term as President of France in the 1980s, Francois Mitterrand was determined to put the Louvre on top. And Foster's transformation of the heart of the British Museum can be understood as a response to the rebuilding of the Louvre by I M Pei. The Louvre, after it had been turned into a public museum in the wake of the French Revolution, was filled with plunder from Napoleon's campaigns. The British, too, were able to acquire exhibits for the Museum by force. The Rosetta Stone was just one of a large number of antiquities seized from the French when Bonaparte surrendered Alexandria.

The biggest physical change in the Museum's history was prompted by another acquisition – the acceptance of the Elgin Marbles by the British government in 1816. So crowded and chaotic had the Museum become that the Marbles had to be accommodated in a temporary prefabricated shed. With the addition of other archaeological artefacts to the collection, the Trustees began to understand that expanding Montagu House was no longer a viable strategy. A new building was inevitable. Sir Robert Smirke, one of the architects retained by the government, was asked to design a suitable structure in 1823. It was the first step in a Europe-wide explosion of museum building.

Leo von Klenze began work on the Glyptothek in Munich in 1816; Karl Friedrich Schinkel designed Berlin's Altes Museum in 1823, though building did not start until 1825. But it was the British Museum, as much as any of the period, that established the classical temple as the archetype for future generations of museums. And given the fact that its greatest treasures were taken from the Parthenon, how could it not have taken its inspiration from that building's austere classicism?

However, despite the impression of permanence that the classical language creates, Smirke's museum has never been static. Its plan, with an open central courtyard, allowed the building to take shape gradually, without ever being closed entirely to visitors. Smirke's museum was twenty-five years in the building. And within seven years of its eventual completion, the open courtyard had been taken over by Panizzi and colonised by the famous circular Reading Room.

For 150 years the Reading Room was one of the sacred sites of world scholarship. It was also a spectacular demonstration of advanced building techniques, with its cast-iron structure, its lightweight papier mâché infill and its concrete foundations. But it concealed the gradual accretion of bookstacks, offices and ancillary spaces that filled up the rest of the courtyard. And the Museum itself, despite the splendour of its front entrance with its Ionic colonnade, lost the clarity of Smirke's original plan.

Opposite: The interior of the Reading Room, photographed in 1925. By the 1930s Sir John Burnett's 1907 redecoration of white and gold had been darkened to a uniform 'elephant grey' by the dank London air.

Above: A reader engrossed in a book, photographed in 1951.

Above: A member of Library staff retrieves a book from one of the closed stacks attached to the drum of the Reading Room, circa 1960.

Opposite: A view of the austere brick drum of the Reading Room and the rooftops of the bookstack buildings massed around it, circa 1943.

Smirke could never have envisaged a museum that would be visited by six million people each year but, had it remained, the courtyard would have been an important means of public orientation. Without that facility, the galleries themselves were turned into circulation routes – choked with visitors using them as corridors to reach one part of the Museum from another.

By the time the Museum launched its architectural competition in 1993, the directorate had spent considerable time thinking about how the space left by the British Library could be used. Foremost among its aims was to return to the Museum the ethnographic collections, which had been relocated in 1970 to the Museum of Mankind. The Museum also needed facilities for schoolchildren and for lectures, together with storage space and accommodation for the shops and cafés that are now an inescapable part of contemporary museum life.

The Reading Room itself was to be sacrosanct. It would become an exhibit in its own right, a pilgrimage site for those who wanted to get a glimpse of the room in which Marx and so many others changed the intellectual history of the world. But it needed a new purpose too: it could not simply be embalmed in a giant glass case, a sad witness to a glorious but now vanished past. Around it, however, the clutter of additions in Smirke's courtyard was of no historical or architectural interest and could be stripped out.

Foster won the competition with a design that was much denser than the scheme he finally built. There was a new glass roof over the courtyard and there was circulation space within it. But the Reading Room was set in a complex of new buildings that would have come much closer to the walls of Smirke's original courtyard.

Foster's competition scheme would not have had the same sense of space, and would have been the poorer for it. It was only once the project was underway that its potential to do more than deal with the mundane round of museum housekeeping and accommodate the husk of the Reading Room became apparent to both the architect and the Museum.

The final scheme extends beyond the limits of the Great Court. It is conceived as a sequence of interlinked elements. The forecourt has been freed from cars and civilised with stone and gravel. The entrance hall has been restored to Smirke's original decorative scheme. The Reading Room is now open to the public for the first time. An education centre has been created, with auditoria, seminar rooms and amenities for parties of schoolchildren. There are new galleries for the ethnographic collections. And, to come, the transformation of the old North Library into the Wellcome Gallery, offering more space for ethnography and potentially the chance to reorganise the north staircase to provide a clear, straight line of access right through the entire Museum.

Foster's design works at three different levels. First, it addresses urban issues. By sinking the galleries and lecture theatres beneath the floor of the courtyard – itself raised up to match the main Museum floor – Foster has freed up space in the courtyard itself. Thus it has become a great urban space – not just the heart of the Museum but related to the city beyond, part of a pedestrian route from Bloomsbury to the Thames.

Visitors can now enjoy a sequence of spaces not so far removed from Smirke's original intentions. They move from the forecourt that he created facing Great Russell Street, through the triumphal colonnade at the front of the Museum, through the richly painted entrance hall into a sudden explosion of light and space beneath the billowing glass and steel roof. From there they may now continue, circulating around the drum of the Reading Room and exiting the Museum on the other side.

Secondly, Foster confronts the issue of how to deal with such an important monument as the British Museum and the extent to which historical authenticity is possible.

The courtyard only existed in its original state for a brief period between 1847 and 1854. According to Panizzi's assistant – who cannot be considered entirely impartial – it was a 'dead loss'. Another critic called it 'the finest mason's yard in Europe'. And the public was excluded from what was by one account, 'a mere well of malaria, a pestilent congregation of vapours'.

The courtyard was once symmetrical, with a portico in the centre of each facade (only the south portico opened onto it, the others being 'blind'). But the south portico was destroyed to extend the entrance hall in 1870, after the Library had opened. Together with the destruction caused by the steady accretion of makeshift additions in the courtyard over the years, the building suffered bomb damage during World War II.

If you are rebuilding architecture with such a complex history, what do you do? How much do you restore? How far do you pretend that new work is in fact old? Smirke had wanted an open courtyard, so in the interests of historical authenticity, do you demolish the Reading Room? Or do you plough the courtyard up, and devote it to growing exotic botanical specimens, as Smirke envisaged? Clearly not.

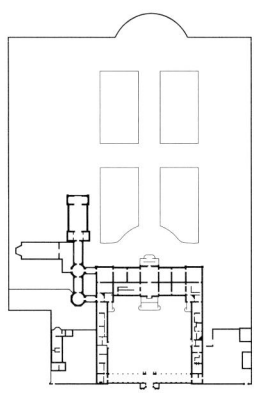

1753

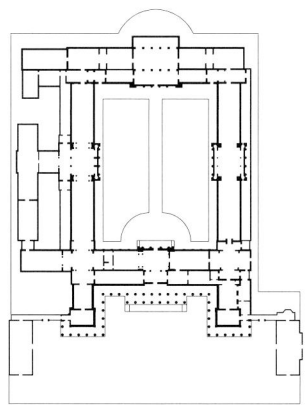

1852

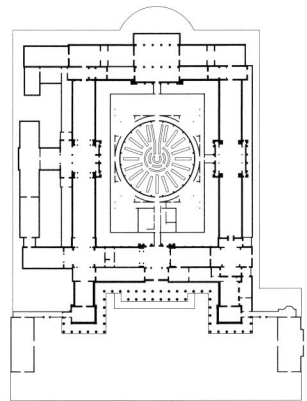

1857

Foster and de Grey believed that, for the Great Court to read as a coherent space, it would be necessary to reconstruct the missing south portico. It is not an exact replica but a new design that reflects contemporary realities. However, much critical comment has focused not on architectural detail but on the precise origin of the stone used to build it. Instead of coming from an English quarry to match the Portland stone of the original, the stone used for the new portico is French.

Historical accuracy has always been a double-edged sword in architectural restoration projects. William Morris established the Society for the Protection of Ancient Buildings to discourage the over-enthusiastic and insensitive restoration of historical buildings, typified by the 'cathedral scrapers' of the mid-nineteenth century. To Morris it was important not to diminish the integrity of the surviving, genuinely ancient fragments of a building. Instead he advocated a strategy of patching and mending, of not pretending that new work was from another period.

In the British Museum it is unrealistic, possibly even undesirable, to expect an exact match between a stone that has spent more than a century in the open air and one that will always exist in a climate-controlled space.

Arguments about the authenticity of the stone, and the difference in colour between the new portico and the wall in which it is placed simply do not stack up. It is important to remember that the courtyard was not built in one go – it took almost twenty-five years to finish. Given the different length of exposure to the elements, the colour of the stone around the courtyard would never have been entirely uniform, and it is not so now. It shows the wear and the scars of the passing of time.

Sooner or later, the stone episode will join the abundant supply of colourful tales that have always been part of the Museum's history. The magnificent entrance front, for example, was built in the 1840s by Baker and Sons, a firm that had not submitted the lowest tender but which, according to Joseph Mordaunt Crook's riveting history of the Museum, had the vital qualification of a managing director married to the architect's sister.

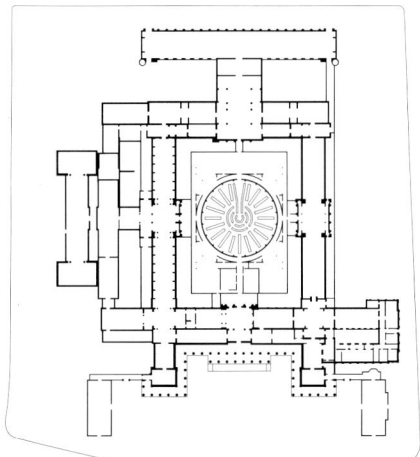

1939

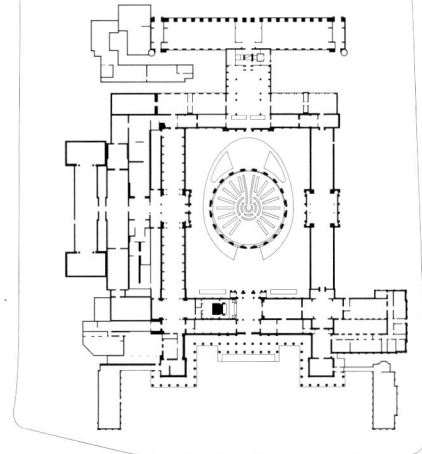

2000

Left: A sequence of plans showing the development of the Museum, from its foundation in Montagu House in 1753 to the present.

Opposite: A new architectural vista — looking up through the skylight of the Reading Room from a vantage point on the floor of the Great Court.

The third key issue that Foster faced was what to do with the external walls of the Reading Room. The building originally had a brick skin, which by the time of the competition had been pierced with modern rectangular window openings. Foster's original plan was to place around the Reading Room a two-storey-high ellipse of accommodation, which would have come to within 7 metres (22.75 feet) of the south portico.

This was modified to become an ovoid, tiered stack of accommodation, which wraps around the circular drum of the Reading Room to the north, accessed via a symmetrical pair of staircases, culminating in a restaurant terrace, level with the pediment of the north portico. The decision was made to face the drum of the Reading Room with limestone, matching the floor of the courtyard. This has the effect of turning the Great Court into a formal, unified space.

The roof was another major element of the design. Its structure is the product of sophisticated analysis carried out in collaboration with engineers Buro Happold, with advice from Chris Williams, a mathematician at Bath University. Because the Reading Room is located eccentrically in the courtyard, no two of the roof's triangular glass panels are exactly the same. And because the drum is not at the centre of a single radiating pattern, the geometry gives the appearance of being non-linear, setting up multiple optical effects that suggest it is closer to the kind of elegant space container envisaged by Buckminster Fuller than to an architectural dome. It also allows the drum of the Reading Room to protrude through it.

The roof is also designed with responsible use of energy for climate control in mind. The ambition was to naturally ventilate the space. Fresh air is supplied through grilles at the edge of the roof and at the main floor level; in winter these can be used to heat the incoming air. The intention is not to climate control the entire volume, just the zone occupied by people.

The completed project is an example of Foster's mature style — a highly accomplished, polished work of architecture, which has the effect of making a hugely complex and difficult project look simple to the point of inevitability. Which is, of course, perhaps the most difficult of architectural tasks.

The Great Court has altered the way that visitors use the Museum. Even when the collections close for the night, the Great Court is alive with activity, open late into the evening as a place to socialise or join in the Museum's continuing intellectual life. You can have a meal or a glass of wine, or go to a lecture or a debate in the auditorium. Or just dwell under that extraordinary roof. It is the nearest a museum can possibly get to creating a real civic space, a covered version of an Italian square, full of people out for an evening stroll.

Foster's interventions have reduced the pressure on the galleries, allowing people to experience the building not only as a series of exhibits, but as a sequence of architectural spaces. However, on the basis of the Museum's past history, this is unlikely to be the last development in the way that it is used.

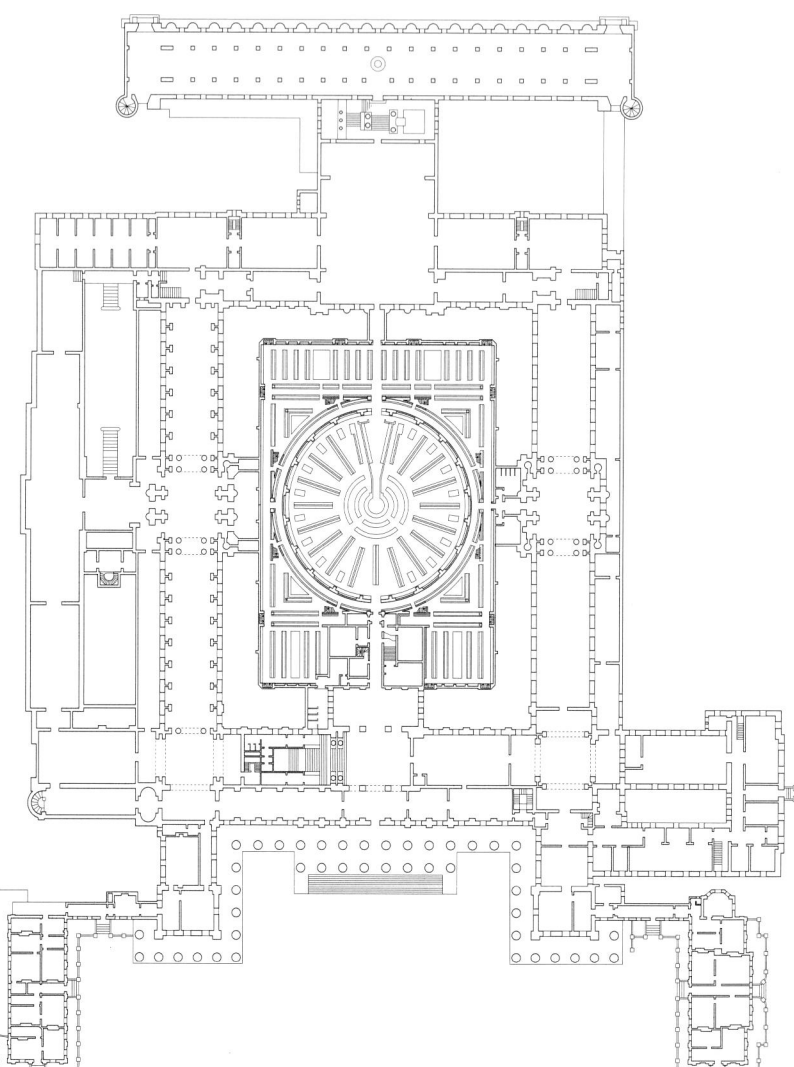

Right: A plan of the British Museum before the creation of the Great Court; the central courtyard is dominated by the Reading Room and almost filled by the rectangle of bookstacks built around it.

Opposite: The plan of the Museum today, to the same scale. the bookstacks have been cleared away and a new public route created through the Museum, focused on the Great Court at its heart.

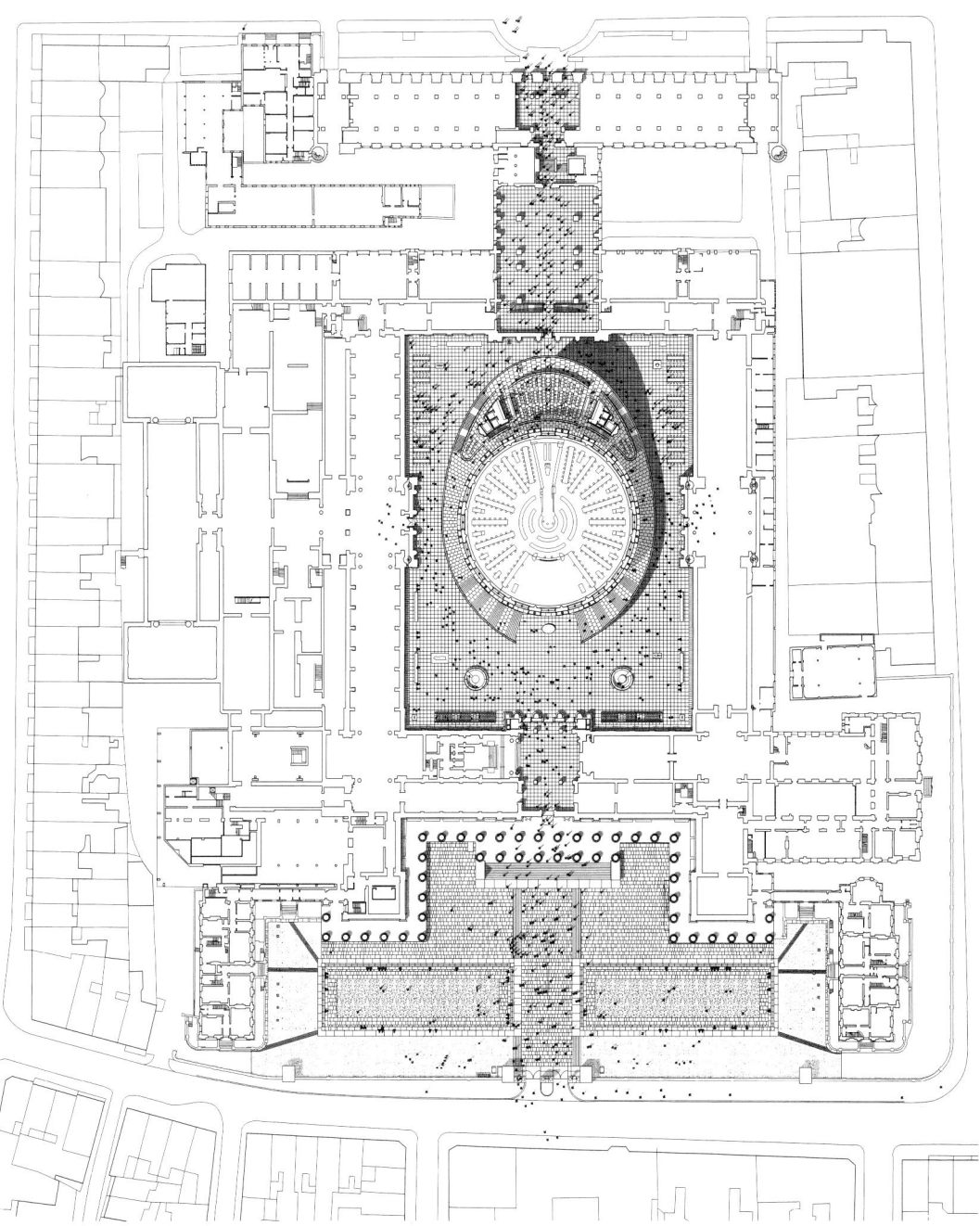

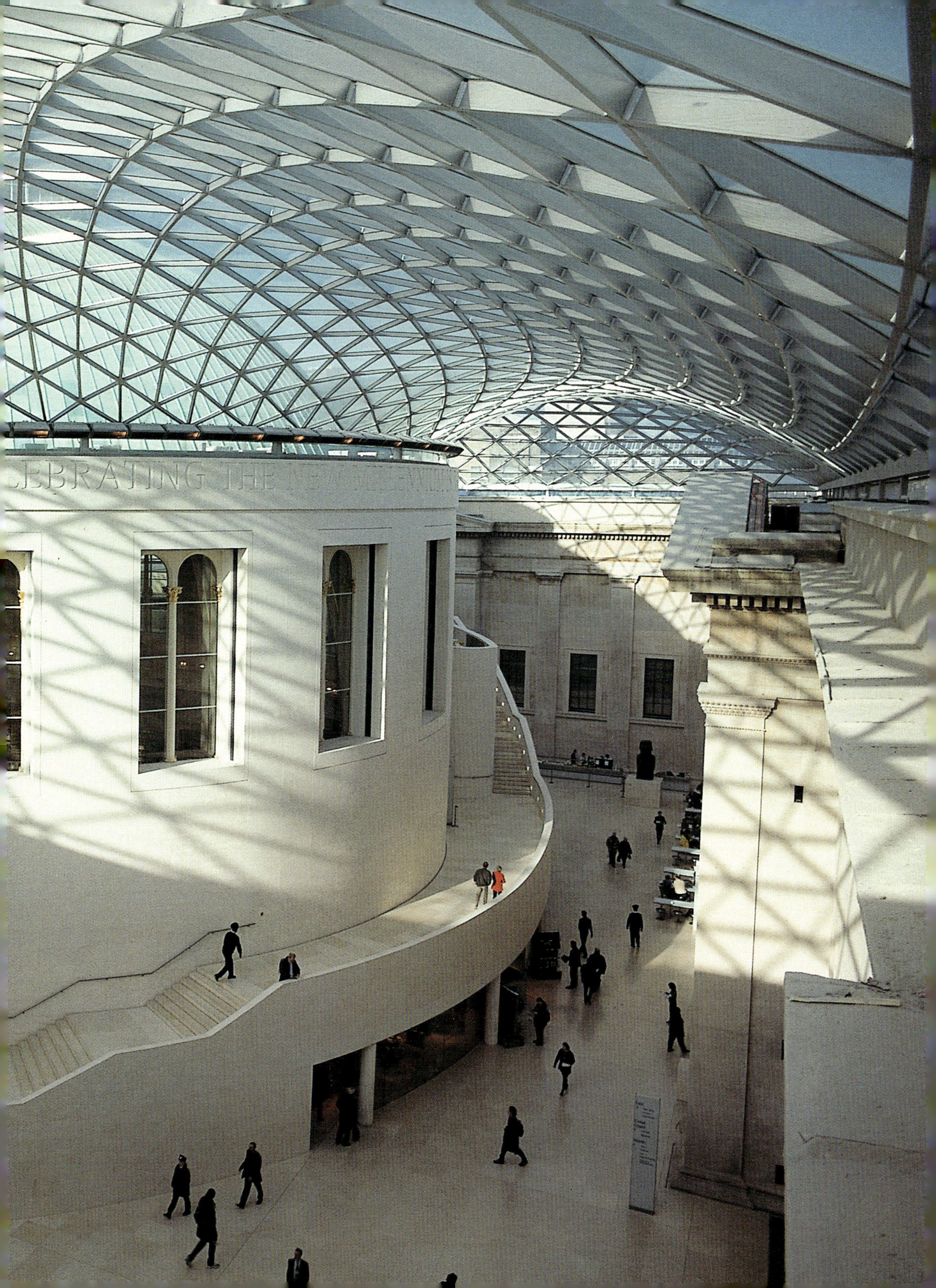
LEBRATING THE

A Project Diary
Spencer de Grey

When in 1993 the British Museum's Trustees announced a competition for the development of the central courtyard, 132 architects from around the world submitted their names to be considered for the project. The following month, in December 1993, the Museum and its advisors selected a shortlist of twenty-two architects, each of whom was asked to describe an approach to the design of the courtyard.

Visiting the British Museum during the competition with Giles Robinson, who was to become our project director, we were immediately struck by how crowded it was. In the nineteenth century Robert Smirke had envisaged around 100,000 visitors a year — but that figure had soared to around six million. The Museum had become a victim of its own popularity. People were being forced to use the galleries themselves as main circulation routes. The result was a confusing and frustrating experience for the visitor.

Below: Scenes from the Museum in the early 1990s, before the creation of the Great Court. People were forced to use the galleries as circulation routes, resulting in a confusing and frustrating experience for the visitor.

The briefing document prepared by the British Museum addressed this issue. Its broad objectives were to provide new and expanded visitor facilities, including an education centre, reception and orientation area, shops and a restaurant. In addition, there was a requirement for galleries to house temporary exhibitions together with elements of the ethnographic collection, which would be returning from Burlington Gardens. The brief was to some extent open to interpretation and allowed the competing firms flexibility as their ideas developed.

Our competition proposals envisaged the Great Court as a new centre for the Museum, a new heart that would remove all the primary circulation from the galleries and open up the possibility of a new public route through the building. The quadrant bookstacks that filled the courtyard were to be demolished, with the restored Reading Room becoming a centre for learning and the focal point of the new Great Court.

The scheme proposed an elliptical structure encapsulating the Reading Room and housing new accommodation on two levels to the north and south. A ramp separated this accommodation from the drum of the Reading Room. Below the main level of the Court we planned space for temporary exhibitions, together with the considerable amount of storage required by the brief. The roof was to be constructed on a square grid supporting transparent inflatable pillows – quite different from the final proposals.

In March 1994 the Museum informed us and two others – Arup Associates and Rick Mather – that we had been selected for a second stage of the competition. Each of us was asked to address a number of issues raised by the first submissions. In May we presented these to the Selection Committee. And on 24 July, the Museum publicly announced the outcome of the competition. We – with engineers Buro Happold and cost consultants Davis Langdon & Everest – had been chosen as the winning team.

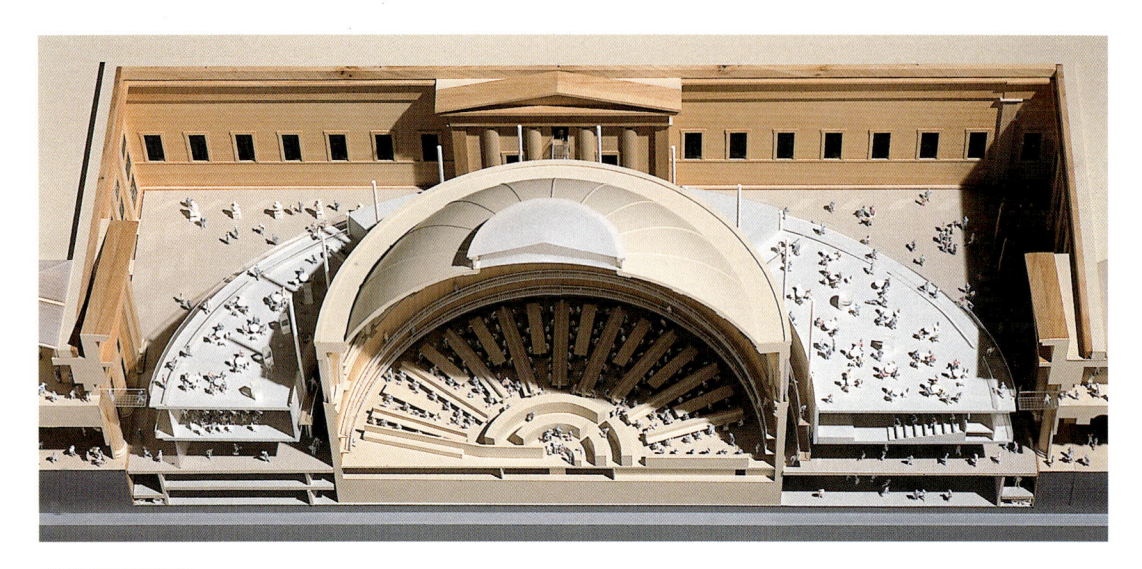

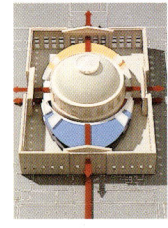

Top left and top far right: Two views of the cut-away model for the second-stage competion scheme, March 1994.

Above: A concept model presented during the first stage of the competition to demonstrate new circulation patterns within the Museum and access from the Great Court into adjacent galleries, January 1994.

The project now began in earnest. The Museum appointed its head of administration, Chris Jones, as the project sponsor, and set up a client committee led by the chairman of the trustees, Graham Greene, which was to be responsible for the project. The director Robert Anderson, joined later by the Museum's new managing director Suzanna Taverne, would also play key roles in the project.

By early 1995, in discussion with the Museum, we had developed the design. Retail space was located beneath the elliptical structure, to the south of the Reading Room, with educational facilities positioned below the main level of the Court. New African Galleries were also located below the Court, to the north. This was made possible by the Museum's decision to relocate storage to a proposed new Study Centre, planned in an old post office building at the other end of Museum Street. At this point the elliptical structure still encircled the Reading Room on both sides and on two levels, linked by a ramp that had now been moved to the outside of this accommodation.

In parallel with the dialogue on the Great Court itself, a much wider strategic discussion about the overall masterplan for the Museum was taking place with Robert Anderson and his team. This highlighted the fact that certain elements of the competition brief could be reduced or relocated elsewhere. Specifically, major temporary exhibitions could be housed by enlarging the existing temporary exhibition galleries, leaving us with the need to provide only a smaller gallery within the Great Court. The same study also showed that the British Museum Society could be rehoused in the south-east wing of the Museum. Thus the amount of accommodation in the Great Court, particularly in the elliptical structure, could be reduced, freeing up more volume. During the second half of 1995, we continued our discussions with English Heritage, the London Borough of Camden and the Royal Fine Art Commission, whose views we incorporated as the design developed.

By the autumn of 1995, the design had changed significantly to reflect these masterplanning studies. The accommodation in the south of the ellipse had been removed and replaced by a double staircase leading to two levels, which were concentrated to the north. For the first time a full-height volume was created in the southern part of the Great Court, linked directly to the main entrance. Instead of three bridges linking the new accommodation to the upper level galleries, there was now only one. All the retail accommodation, together with the café serveries, was contained within what was now an ovoid structure to the north of the Reading Room. The temporary exhibition gallery was placed at the first-floor level of this structure. Above it we placed the restaurant. Access to both these levels was via a stepped ramp. Beneath the Great Court, the accommodation was much the same as finally built.

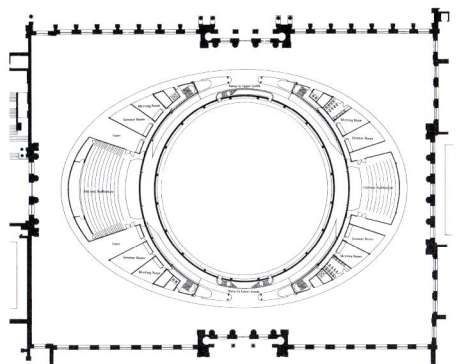

Above: Plan of the education centre level, accommodating two auditoria and seminar and meeting rooms, as proposed at the second stage of the competition, March 1994.

41

At this point we were proposing the use of stepped ramps versus the more usual staircase. We also looked at hydraulic lifts rather than traction lifts in order to minimise the appearance of the lift cores as they emerged at the uppermost level. Both these topics were the subject of hot debate within the Museum. Whilst approval was given for hydraulic lifts, ultimately we were unable to find a convincing solution with the stepped ramp and so we opted instead for stairs.

The reconstruction of Smirke's south portico, demolished when the entrance hall was extended into the courtyard in the nineteenth century, was an important feature of the scheme, one that also underwent considerable design development. Smirke's Ionic portico originally had a domestically proportioned doorway. The projected annual influx of at least six million visitors meant that we would have to provide a more generous entrance. In the competition scheme we proposed the reconstruction of the portico's columns and pilasters without the ashlar masonry walls that originally stood between them. However, in discussion with English Heritage and the Heritage Lottery Fund's advisors, we decided to reinstate the walls, punctuating them with three large doorways, in order to preserve the unity of the portico and achieve a stronger relationship between the south portico and the other facades.

Below: Plans at auditorium level, courtyard level, Hotung Gallery level and restaurant level, from left to right respectively; as submitted for planning approval, December 1995.

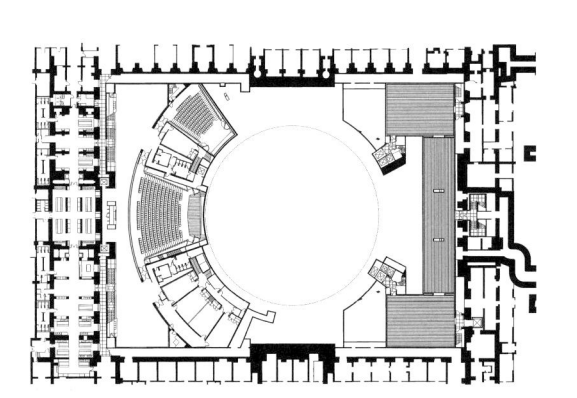

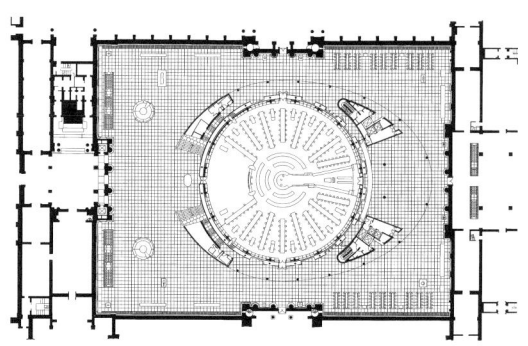

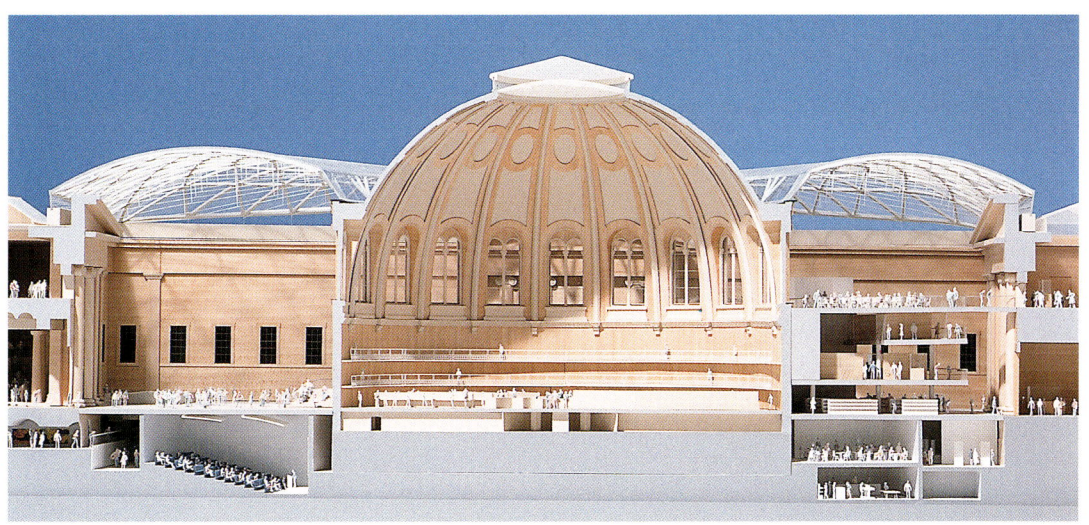

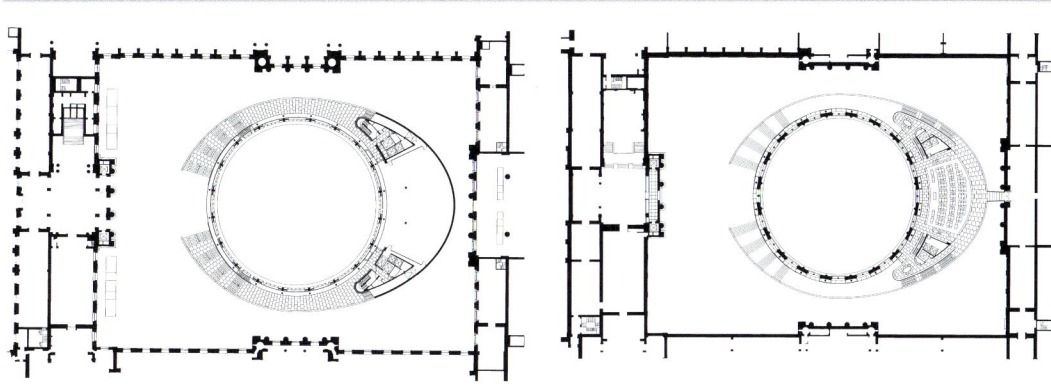

The new portico is a reinvention of Smirke's original design. It stands further forward in the courtyard in order to accommodate two new lifts that provide access to all the Museum's public levels. We also added an attic window in the central bay to afford spectacular views into the Great Court from the Central Saloon, which is located on the upper level immediately behind the south portico. Interestingly, the provenance for such an opening was to be found in one of Smirke's original sketches.

Top: View of the sectional model as submitted for planning approval in December 1995. The roof is approaching its final form, but the geometry has still to be resolved.

The door leading into the Reading Room, which faces visitors as they enter the Great Court from the south, posed a similar challenge. When it was built, its height was limited by the position of the balcony structure within. Hitherto this had never been an issue: historically the Reading Room had been reached through a relatively narrow, low-ceilinged passageway. But once this had been removed and the scale of the doorway could be gauged in the context of the new space, it appeared disproportionately small.

We looked at a variety of formal solutions. One was to create a larger symbolic doorway within which the existing door would sit. This could take the form of inscribed stone panels – a concept that was then completely modelled. The idea of signalling an entrance in this manner is a long-standing tradition. However, over time we decided to seek a more contemporary solution, which led to the decision to commission the sculptor Anish Kapoor to make a sculpture to mark the Reading Room entrance. His initial proposal was a concave polished stainless-steel dish that leant against the drum of the Reading Room. In its final form this has become a concave elongated ellipse and is cantilevered from the floor structure.

The glazed roof that forms a protective net high above the Great Court allows the space to be used throughout the day and in all weathers. From the outset we wanted the roof structure to be visually as delicate and minimal as possible. We also wanted to allow the optimum amount of daylight into the Great Court, so creating the sensation of being in an outdoor space.

The canopy of inflated ETFE (ethylenetetrafluoroethylene) 'pillows' that we investigated during the competition stage and for some time afterwards, consisted of two layers of a translucent plastic foil filled with air, supported on a regular diagonal grid, 4.3 metres (14 feet) square. This material has some benefits over glass, chief amongst them its availability in large sheets, which would have enabled us to span greater distances. The system also has excellent thermal characteristics because of the trapped air in the pillows, and the pillows could have been constructed with interlayers to block ultra-violet radiation.

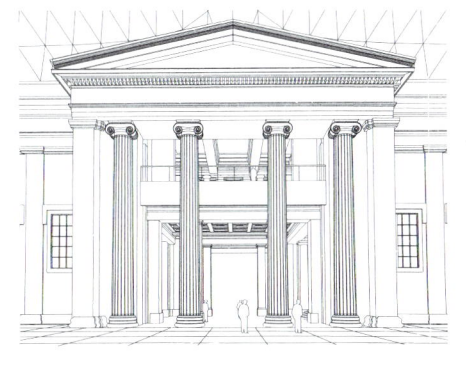

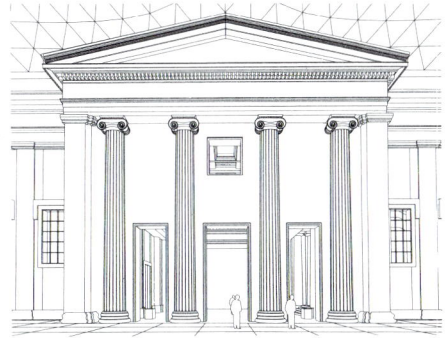

Opposite and centre left: Two views of the reinstated south portico as it was first envisaged, shown from the entrance hall and Great Court respectively. The columns would have been reinstated but without the walls between, allowing the Central Saloon to open out onto the Great Court, October 1995.

Below left: A plan of the new south portico and entrance hall as first conceived, October 1995.

Left: The south portico reconceived: ashlar masonry walls are reinstated between the columns and an attic window allows views from the Central Saloon into the Great Court, March 1997.

Top left: A view of the Great Court's south portico as built.

Paradoxically, however, the inherent lightness of the ETFE foil required a heavy steel structure to resist uplift in strong winds. The size of the foil panels might have allowed us to use fewer structural members than would be required by smaller panes, but the members themselves would have had to be much thicker to provide the necessary weight. Eventually we decided that, although such a solution might be appropriate in many locations, it did not sit well with the classical architecture of the courtyard. The pillows lacked the sense of quality, elegance and permanence for which we were looking – the roof had to be glass.

As we began to investigate the alternatives we quickly realised that square glass panels would be inappropriate to resolve the irregular space between the courtyard facades and the drum of the Reading Room, and so we pursued a triangulated structure. But there were still many challenges to be met.

The roof had to cover an area measuring 100 by 70 metres (325 by 227 feet) and span lengths varying from 14 metres (45.5 feet), where the Reading Room is closest to the courtyard's facades, to 40 metres (130 feet) at the corners of the courtyard. And it had to be vaulted in order to clear the porticoes at the centre of each facade but it also had to be shallow enough to minimise the visual impact on the streets surrounding the Museum.

The situation was further complicated by the fact that the Reading Room is not located at the centre of the courtyard, but is 5 metres (16.25 feet) closer to the north facade. Resolving this irregular geometry would take many months and require a state-of-the-art, form-generating computer programme, which we developed in close collaboration with Mike Cook and Steve Brown from Buro Happold together with Chris Williams, a mathematician at Bath University.

The resulting form is generated from a grid of radial elements spanning between the circle of the Reading Room and the rectangle of the courtyard, which are interconnected by two opposing spirals so that the roof works as a shell. The intersections create triangular spaces, which are filled with glazing.

Initially, the triangles were much bigger than they appear in the final design and they generated irregular residual shapes around the perimeter, at the junction with the Reading Room and the courtyard walls. At one point in the design process, we were considering using as many as 10,664 triangular panels, compared to the 3,312 that make up the final smooth-flowing geometry you see today.

Between late 1995 and the summer of 1996 we also worked on developing a system that would minimise the roof's steelwork by integrating the main structural elements with the fixings and support for the glass. We began with structural members with a circular hollow section, which supported an independent glazing system. These studies continued for some time – we investigated many different cross-sections together with a glazing system with bolted fixings. But finally we arrived at an integrated structural and glazing system that employs rectangular hollow steel sections. This was the basis of the design tendered and constructed by Waagner Biro from Vienna – the firm that built the Reichstag's new cupola – under the direction of Johann Sischka.

As built, the roof weighs almost 800 tonnes: 478 tonnes of steel and 315 tonnes of glass. It is supported on 11 kilometres (6.8 miles) of steel members and consists of 5,162 purpose-made steel box beams that intersect at 1,826 unique structural six-way nodes.

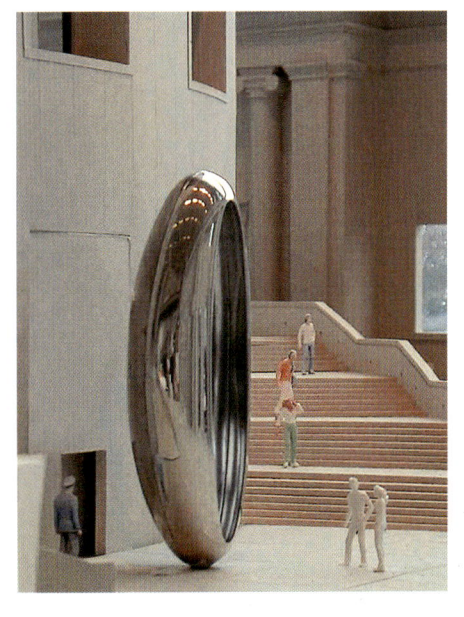

Above and far left: Norman Foster and Anish Kapoor discuss the installation and positioning of Kapoor's sculpture and its integration within the Great Court. A model of Kapoor's earlier proposal for a disc-shaped form can be seen on the table, April 2000.

Left: A model of the Kapoor sculpture, showing its final position in the Great Court in front of the entrance to the Reading Room.

47

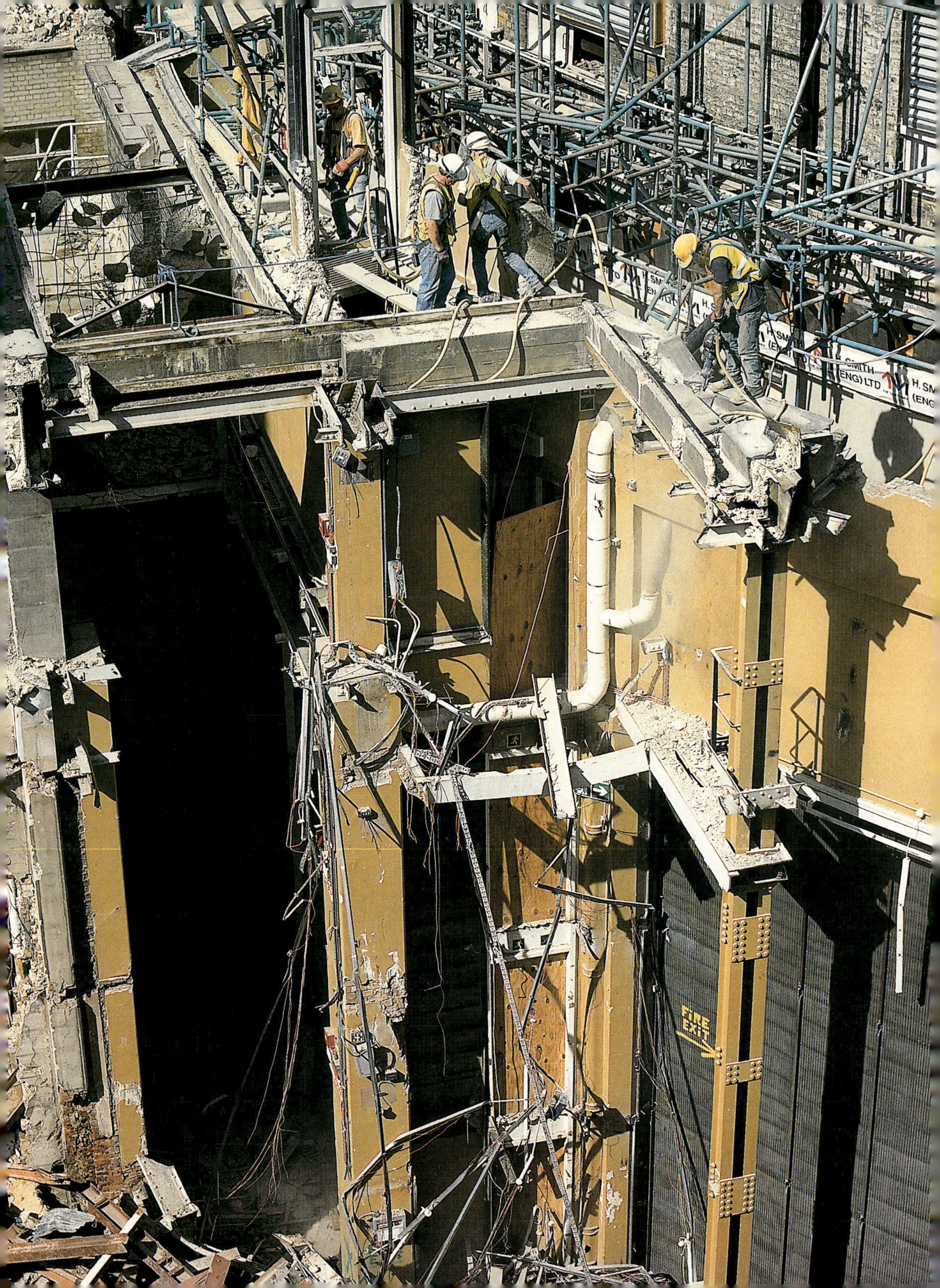
FIRE EXIT

The double-glazing system, with its toughened outer layer and laminated inner layer, allows daylight to filter through and illuminate the courtyard, passing into the Reading Room and, in very controlled quantities, into the surrounding galleries. In order to reduce solar heat gain the tinted glass panels are screen-printed with small reflective dots over 56 per cent of their surface – a technique known as 'fritting'. As a result 75 per cent of the sun's heat – as infra-red radiation – is prevented from entering the Court.

So that the roof's supporting structure should not obscure the newly restored courtyard facades, the roof has been designed as a single-span structure – there are no visible columns or supporting elements within the Great Court itself. It is supported only at its edges and at the centre, around the drum of the Reading Room.

At its junction with the Reading Room the roof is supported on a ring of twenty new columns, which align with the historical structure's cast-iron frame. These carry the weight of the roof down to the foundations ensuring that no additional load is applied to the Reading Room structure. The columns are tubular steel filled with concrete and are slender enough to be hidden behind the Reading Room's new stone cladding, which also provides space for vertical services risers containing rainwater pipes, ventilation ducts and the like. Around the Reading Room, the roof is prevented from spreading sideways by a new reinforced-concrete snow gallery (a structure that rings the dome and was originally designed to 'break the fall' of heavy loads of snow from the roof). This structure replaced an existing brick arched gallery. It acts as a stiffening diaphragm, balancing the thrusts from opposite sides of the roof, and is supported on sliding bearings, which allow the rigid ring beam to float above the historical frame.

At the outer perimeter the roof rests on Smirke's original load-bearing masonry walls, connected by short steel columns to a new reinforced-concrete parapet beam. To avoid applying any sideways load to the quadrangle buildings, the roof is supported on sliding bearings. These allow the structure to move naturally, responding to changes in temperature or the weight of snow for example, and spread the loads vertically through the courtyard's facades. Large forces are generated by the abrupt change in direction at the corners of the roof and the structure is stiffened in these areas by a tension cable across each corner.

Enclosing the Great Court with a glazed roof also raised a number of environmental issues. Working with Neil Billet of Buro Happold we strove to resolve these in an ecologically friendly way. Wherever possible we wanted to use natural ventilation. This is provided in the Great Court by high and low-level grilles positioned around the edge of the space. These grilles introduce filtered fresh air into the courtyard at the main floor level. As the air warms it rises naturally within the space and is expelled via the high-level grilles, which are discreetly located behind the stone parapets. The stone floor in the courtyard is warmed in the winter and cooled in the summer by means of water pipes below the stone. This allows the temperature in the Great Court to be maintained between a minimum of 18°C in winter and a maximum of 25°C in summer. In the remainder of the new spaces full air-conditioning is supplied via four secondary plant rooms located beneath the Court.

Opposite: With the last book from the British Library removed from the Museum, demolition of the quadrangle bookstacks could begin, March 1998. A total of 20,000 cubic metres of material would be removed over the course of the next nine months.

In December 1995, a planning and listed building application was submitted to the London Borough of Camden. This was approved in January 1997. Early in 1997 MACE was appointed as construction manager to coordinate the forty contractors for the project; Carl Wright would lead their team on site; Reg Cobham was brought in to stengthen the Museum's management team.

As the design team continued to develop and refine the proposals for the project, the Museum and the departing British Library had the Herculean task of vacating the buildings that stood in the courtyard. Throughout 1997 over three million books were removed from the Library, including rare and fragile manuscripts, a laborious task given the restricted access to the courtyard. While this was happening the Museum began the process of decommissioning and, in some instances, rebuilding facilities that would be lost, including the rifle range in the eastern basement, home to the Museum's gun club – the oldest in Great Britain.

By March 1998 the last book had left the Reading Room. By now the Museum's Development Trust, under the direction of Sir Claus Moser, had received many major donations – including one from the Millennium Commission and one from the Heritage Lottery Fund – and was quietly confident of the financial position. Demolition of the quadrant bookstacks could begin!

Demolition was a complex, arduous task, which took more than nine months to complete. It was made more complicated by the fact that there was no direct access into the courtyard – everything had to be lifted in or out by two cranes, one of which had a 75-metre jib – the longest of its kind in Europe.

As the old buildings gradually came down, the courtyard facades were uncovered for the first time in over 140 years. Many unforeseen problems began to emerge, the most notable being the extensive damage to the masonry columns of the east, west and north porticoes inflicted by the Victorians as they raced to complete the quadrant bookstacks in the 1850s. We were also struck by the indifferent appearance of the exterior of the Reading Room with its utilitarian brickwork and metal-framed windows.

By October 1998 the majority of the bookstack buildings had been taken down to ground level, some 3 metres (10 feet) lower than the floor-level of the surrounding galleries. Many thousands of tonnes of demolition materials – sufficient to fill twelve Olympic-size swimming pools – had been removed from the site.

Before excavation works could commence, however, it was necessary to stabilise parts of the Reading Room and the courtyard facades. Using a process called jet grouting, concrete was injected at high pressure beneath the existing structures to form new foundations. This was a finely balanced operation that required the cast- and wrought-iron frame of the Reading Room's 4,200 tonne dome to be monitored constantly, second by second, for structural movement to ensure that no adverse stresses were being placed upon it.

Top left, top right and right: As the delicate process of demolition continued during 1998 the outer shell of the Reading Room came to light for the first time in 140 years. It was revealed as very plain in contrast to the elaborately decorated interior.

Above: When the quadrangle facades emerged it became apparent that they had been severely damaged in the nineteenth century when the Reading Room and associated buildings were constructed.

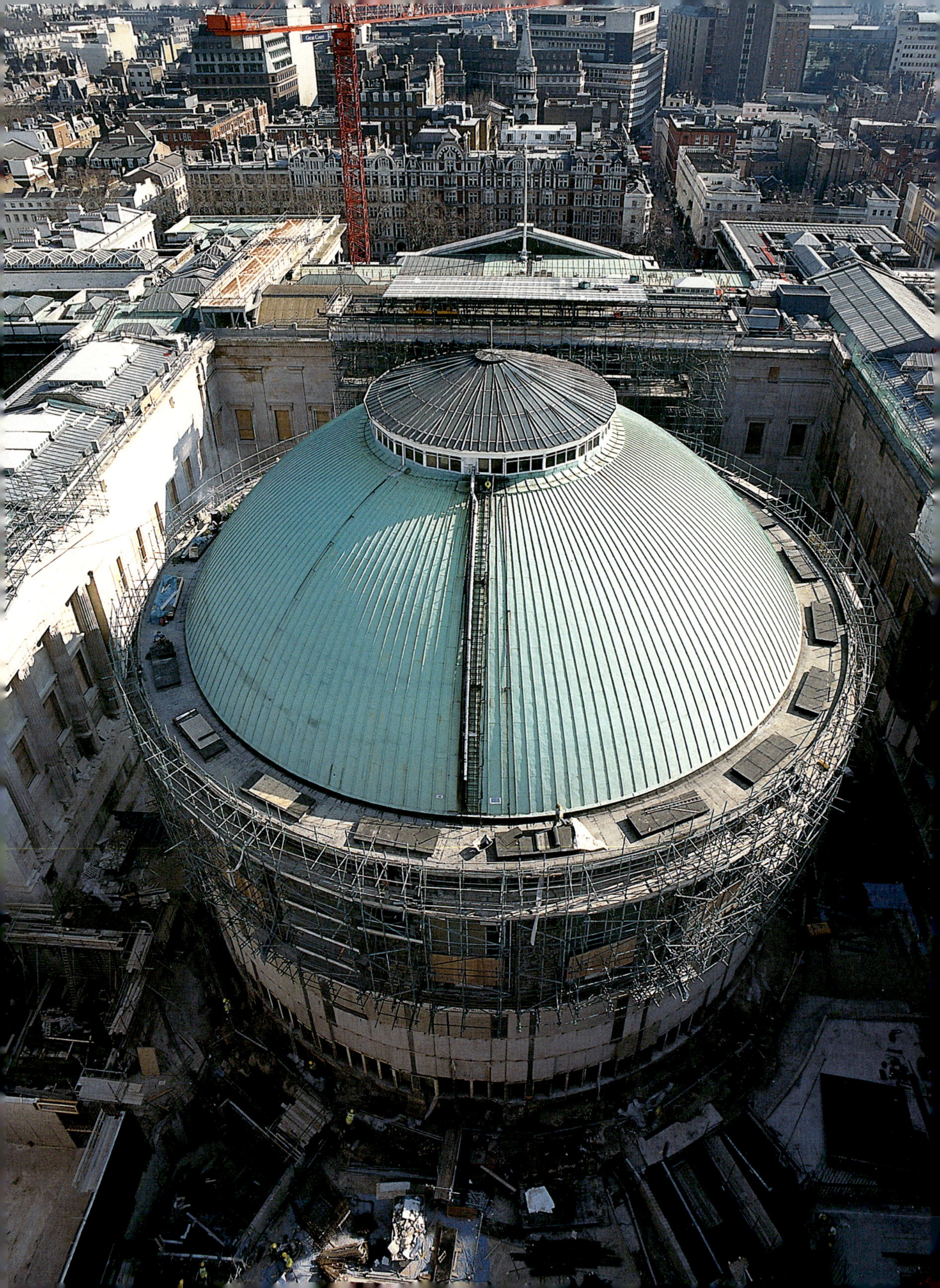

Opposite: An aerial
view of the site,
looking south,
March 1999.

Above: Norman
Foster and Spencer
de Grey inspect
progress on site,
September 1999.

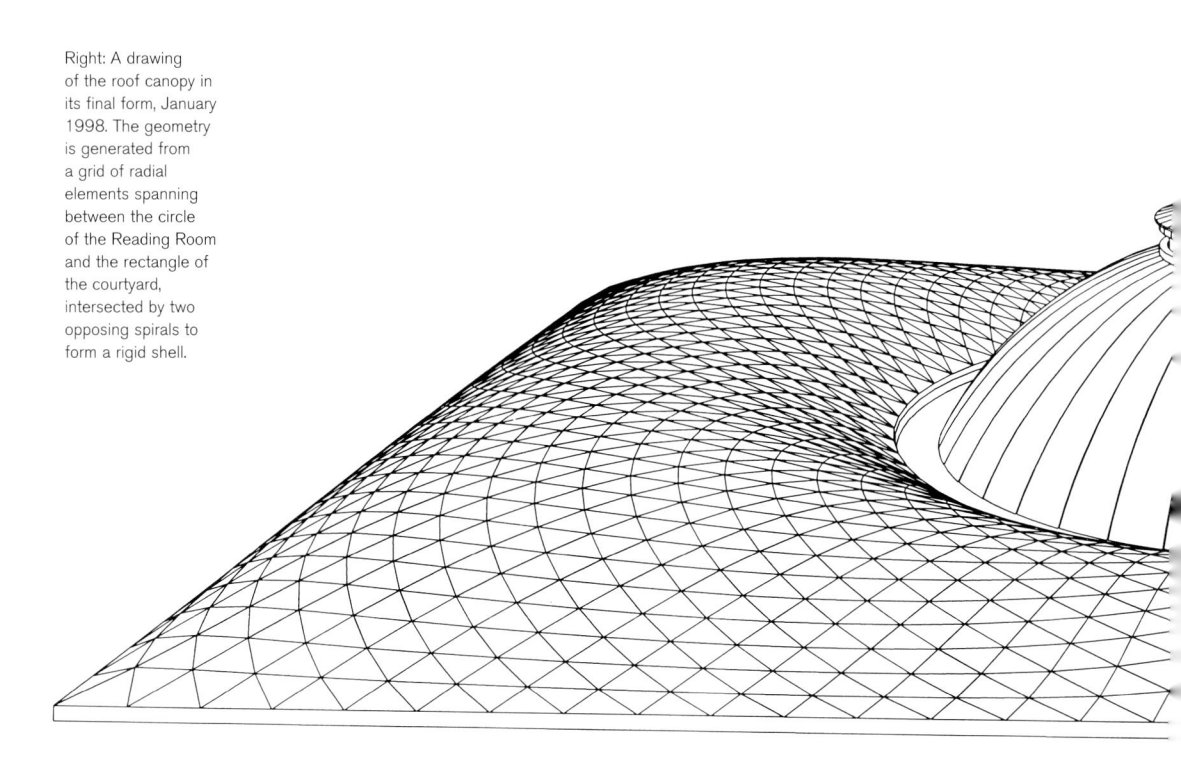

Right: A drawing of the roof canopy in its final form, January 1998. The geometry is generated from a grid of radial elements spanning between the circle of the Reading Room and the rectangle of the courtyard, intersected by two opposing spirals to form a rigid shell.

Above: An aerial view of the Museum showing the completed roof in context; its smooth form comprises 3,312 triangular glazed panels, each of unique dimensions and profile.

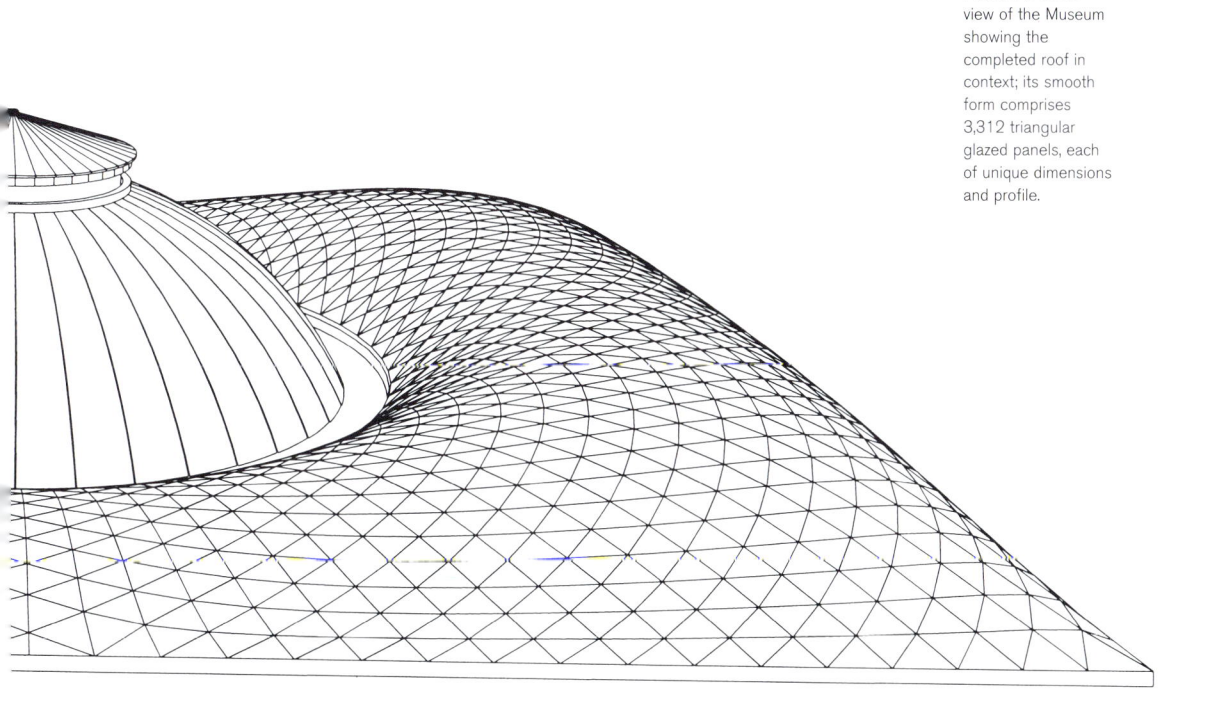

Right: Detail at the perimeter of the Great Court; the roof sits on sliding bearings to allow differential movement between the steel structure and the masonry walls on which it bears. The roof is supported with the minimum intervention to the existing structure. As a result it appears almost to float. This section also shows the extent to which the new south portico projects into the Great Court, creating space for two new liftshafts.

Opposite: Detail at the junction of the roof and the Reading Room. The inner rim off the roof is supported on twenty columns concealed in the void between the new Reading Room cladding and the line of the original structure.

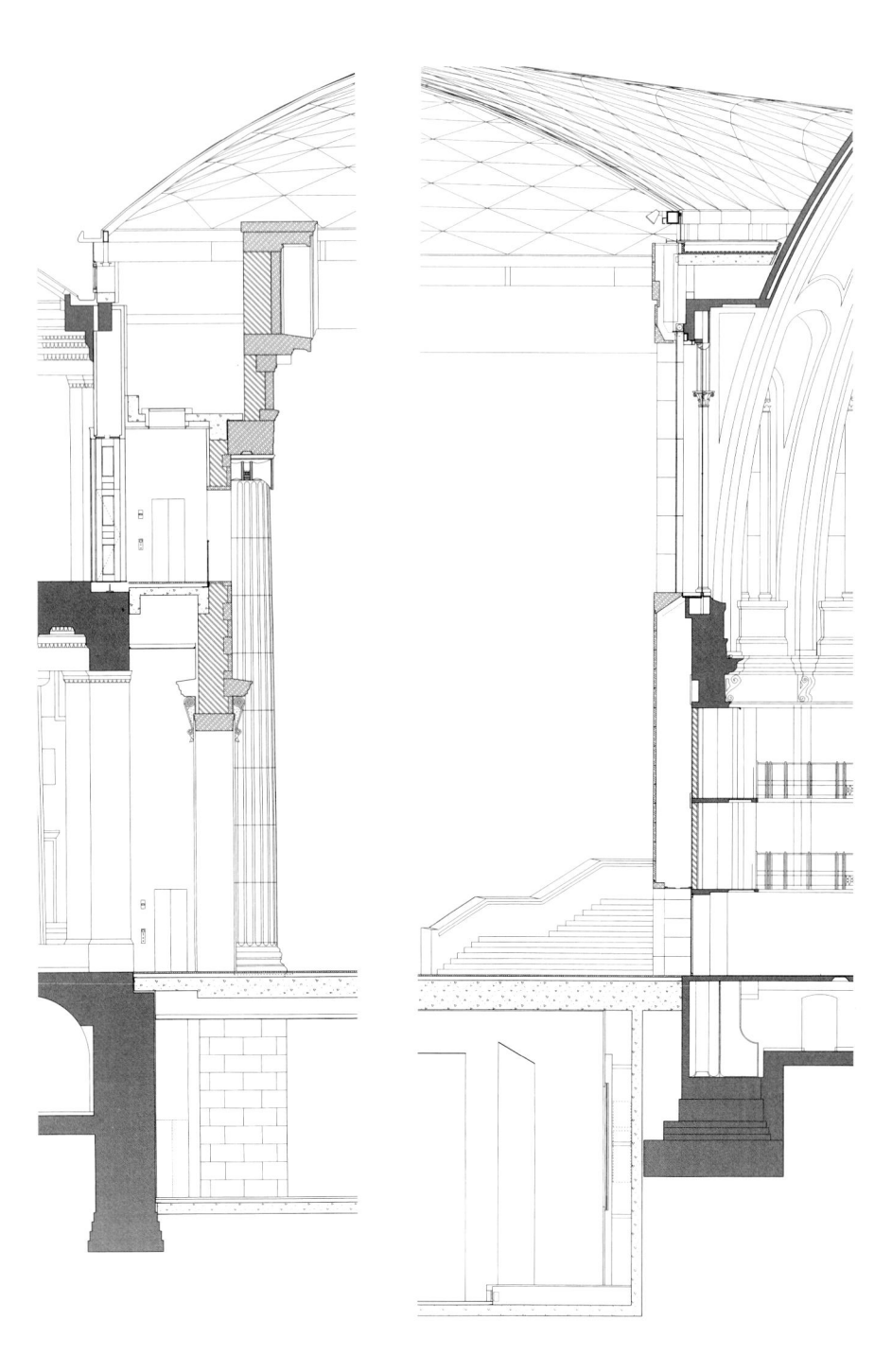

With the Reading Room structure and Smirke facades stabilised, excavation works could begin. This was a slow process, made difficult by the fact that the lowest levels of excavation were below the water-table and therefore needed to be drained continually. As the ground material was removed, the Portland stone facades gave way to Smirke's massive brick and concrete foundations. Standing at the foundation level, the sheer scale of these walls became apparent. The battered, austere Greek Revival masonry rose cliff-like some 23 metres (75 feet) out of the ground.

Meanwhile the design and construction teams were finalising their proposals and tendering some forty separate trade packages. These packages of work varied significantly, from the massive concrete works of the basement structures, to the intricate, specialised decorative gilding to be undertaken in the Reading Room, and the highly sophisticated technologies of steel and glass manufacture deployed in the roof structure.

As the new Great Court floor structure began to emerge, the race was on to find and install some 60 kilometres (37.5 miles) of scaffold pole to construct a temporary deck within the Great Court. This would form the 'ground' from which the roof structure would be built. Equivalent in size to Hanover Square and raised 18 metres (58.5 feet) in the air – the equivalent of six stories above pavement level – it was a heroic undertaking in itself.

In the meantime, around the four Smirke facades, teams of stone conservators were busy restoring the damaged stonework, generating large quantities of masonry dust in the process. An important element of this restoration was the reconstruction of the south portico. The portico alone required 1,000 tonnes of load-bearing stone and was built using traditional construction techniques, which Smirke would have recognised. Work started on site in April 1999 and was completed in January 2000, an impressive achievement given that the stones weighed up to 7 tonnes each.

Whilst this frenetic activity was taking place around them, Ian Bristow and Richard Ireland were expertly and painstakingly restoring the interior of the Reading Room dome and the original decorative scheme in the front entrance hall.

By May 1999 the northern half of the Great Court had been enclosed by the construction deck, which created a vast subterranean world of scaffold poles, dimly lit construction materials and ubiquitous masonry dust. From the construction deck the new roof structure could now be formed, supported on the scaffolding below.

Throughout the entire construction period the Museum remained open to the public as usual. The only access to the site was by crane, and this inevitably placed restrictions on the size of the components that could be used to construct the roof.

Right: The roof was constructed from a series of pre-assembled, ladder-like sections, which were transported to site over a period of six months, November 1999.

Below: Individual ladder sections were supported on a network of temporary props and welded together on site, August 1999.

Above: With the roof nearly complete the temporary construction deck from which it was assembled is taken down, April 2000.

Below: The last of the roof's glazed panels is ceremoniously fitted into place, 13 July 2000.

Above: With most of the glazing in place, Spencer de Grey, Suzanna Taverne and representatives from Buro Happold and MACE remove the last of 593 temporary roof supports, 13 April 2000.

In the months before work began on site, thousands of steel elements had been manufactured by Waagner Biro in Vienna and shipped to Derby for pre-assembly into a series of ladder-like sections. Over a period of six months these elements were craned over the Museum buildings onto the site. The construction deck became a vast sorting office with unique steel elements carefully coded and stored in groups ready for erection onto a precise system of temporary props. A team of welders then joined the individual ladders together to form the main structural grid. The logistics of this process were all-important if the tight construction programme was to be achieved. In all the roof was to take fourteen months to erect.

The successful connection of the thousands of individual steel components was critical to the integrity of the roof structure. To minimise the risks of welding failure, an extremely high grade of steel was used – one that is more typically used for marine, or petrochemical applications than for buildings. Furthermore, because the steel structure was built to an accuracy of plus or minus 3 millimetres ($1/_8$ inch), the impurities present in lower-grade steel would have allowed too great a margin for error.

We chose steel for the structure because it provides high strength and stiffness at relatively low cost. It is capable of absorbing high stresses and can be produced in the most slender of forms. It is also easily connected by bolting or welding and, with a surface coating, has excellent weathering characteristics.

The assembly process was complicated by the fact that the resulting steel lattice had to be built higher than the roof's projected final profile in order to allow the structure to deflect up to 150 millimetres (6 inches) when the glass cladding was fixed in place. The glass panels were fixed into position in a pre-arranged sequence, in order to ensure that the roof deflected in accordance with the engineers' mathematical models.

By the late spring of 2000 the structural lattice was complete and the majority of the glass had been installed, which meant that the temporary scaffolding could be removed. As the roof was systematically 'de-propped' the structure dropped 150 millimetres (6 inches) in height and spread 90 millimetres (3.5 inches) laterally as it settled onto its sliding bearings and became self-supporting. Throughout this process the roof structure was precisely monitored using specialised surveying equipment to ensure that it behaved as predicted by the engineers. Thus its complex geometry was translated from design into reality.

We celebrated the installation of the last pane of glass on 13 July – a duty performed jointly by my young daughter, Georgia, and Joe Homden, son of the Museum's director of public affairs, Carol Homden.

The finishing touches within the courtyard included the fit-out of the shops and restaurant, the installation of sculptures such as the Lion of Knidos, which weighs over 7 tonnes, and the execution of the wall and floor inscriptions.

The pressure was now on the finishing trades to commence their works. These involved the installation of the under-floor heating and cooling system, the cladding of the Reading Room drum, and the laying of some 5,000 square metres (54,000 square feet) of stone flooring. While these works progressed in sequence from north to south the final elements of the roof were being completed.

Finally, on 6 December 2000 – some thirty-three months after construction began – the Great Court was opened officially by Her Majesty the Queen. The combined efforts of the client, the consultants and the construction team had delivered the project on time and within the original budget, without ever closing the Museum.

Above: Views of the roof under construction looking north from the vantage point of the construction crane in the Museum forecourt, taken in March 1999, January, February and April 2000 respectively.

1998
An aerial view of the Museum looking south, taken shortly before construction of the Great Court roof began.

2000
The corresponding view after completion of the glazed canopy over the Great

Above: A close-up view of the roof glazing showing the ceramic frits that are printed over its surface to reduce glare and solar gain.

Opposite: An exploded assembly drawing showing how the glazing panels and the elements of the structural frame fit together.

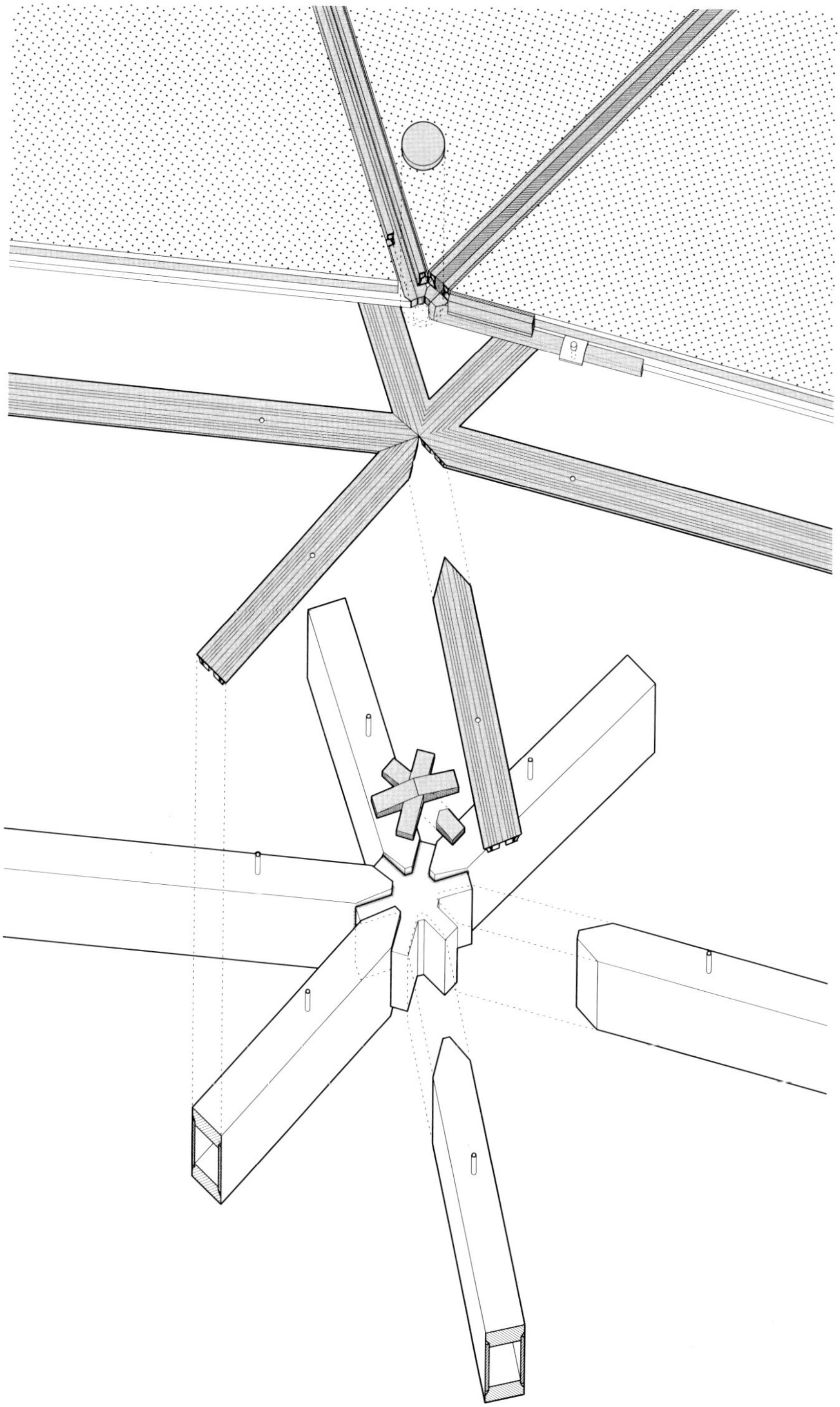

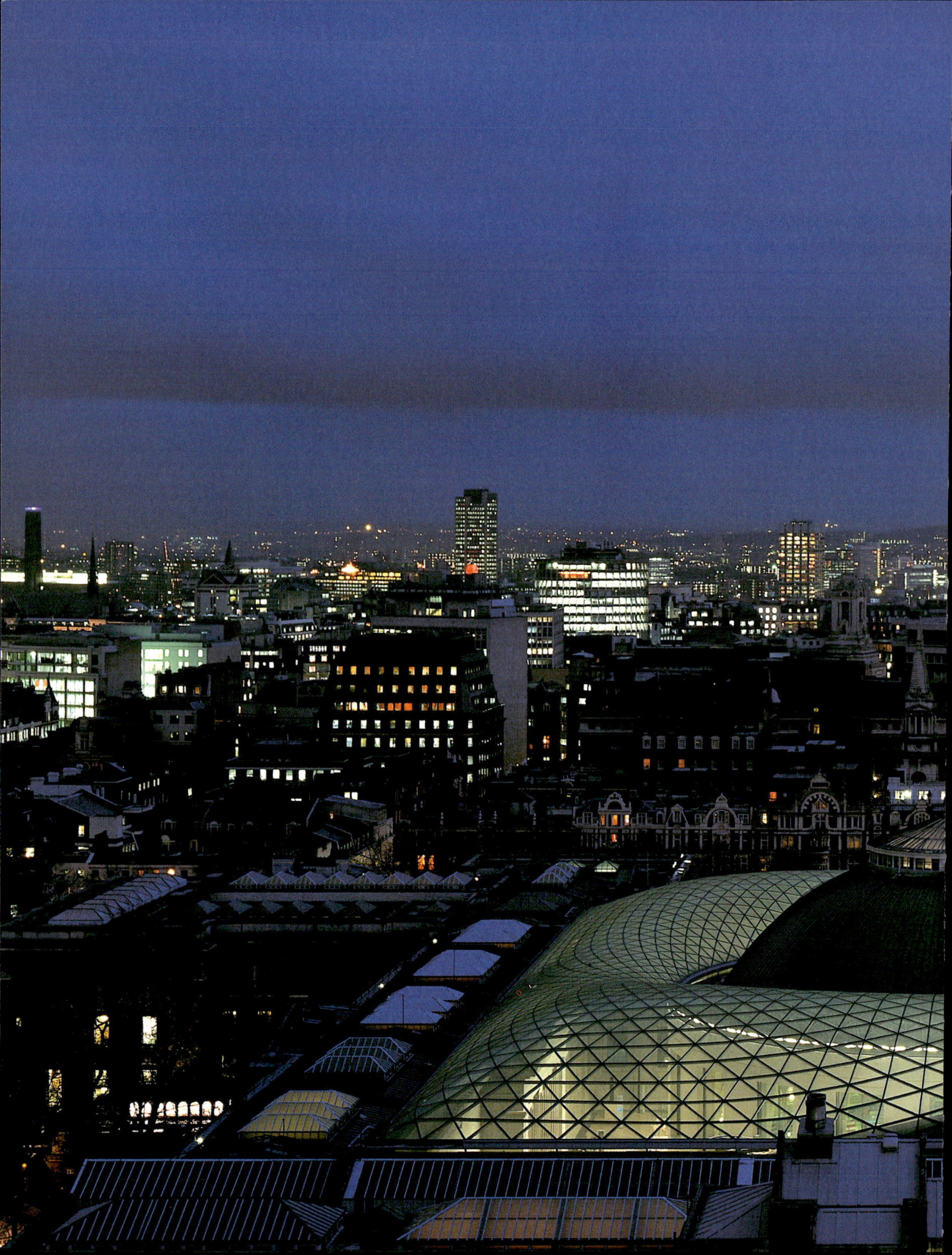

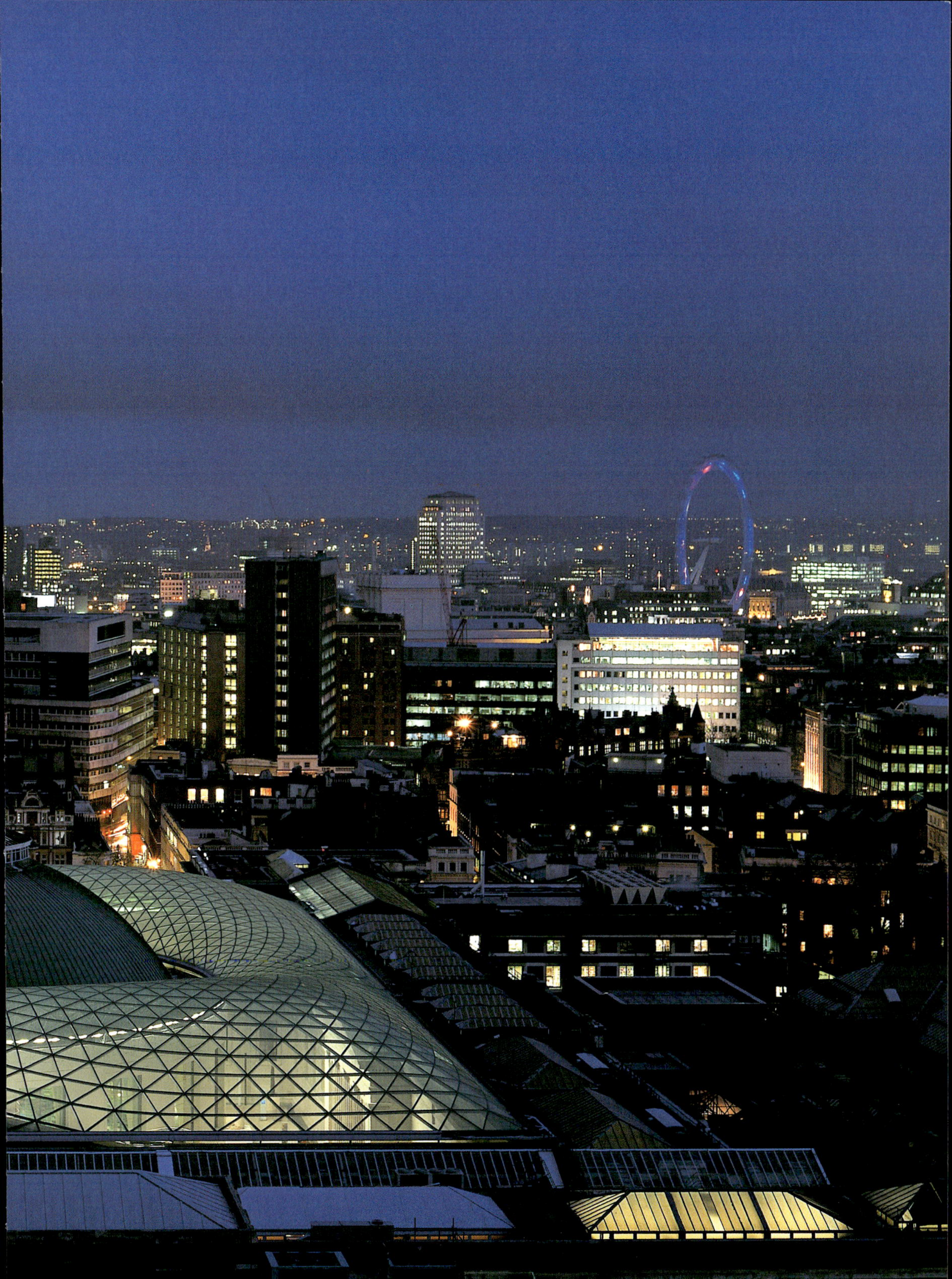

Elements of the Great Court

The Great Court is today the largest enclosed civic space in Europe, similar in size to many of London's public squares. Entering either from the south or the north, it is now possible to walk through the heart of the Museum from Bloomsbury to Covent Garden and beyond as part of a new pedestrian route from the Euston Road to the South Bank.

Although popular attention is focused on the Great Court, the project in fact comprises eight linked elements. In addition to the Great Court itself these are: the reinstatement of the Museum's forecourt; the restoration of the entrance hall; the refurbishment of the Reading Room; the creation of the Clore Education Centre and the Ford Centre for Young Visitors; the Sainsbury African Galleries for Ethnography and, finally, the Wellcome Gallery – also for Ethnography – which will be completed in 2003.

Left: An exploded axonometric of the Great Court showing how the various elements of the scheme are arranged in relation to the Museum's main floor level. Beneath the Great Court to the south are the Clore Education Centre and the Ford Centre for Young Visitors, with the Sainsbury African Galleries to the north.

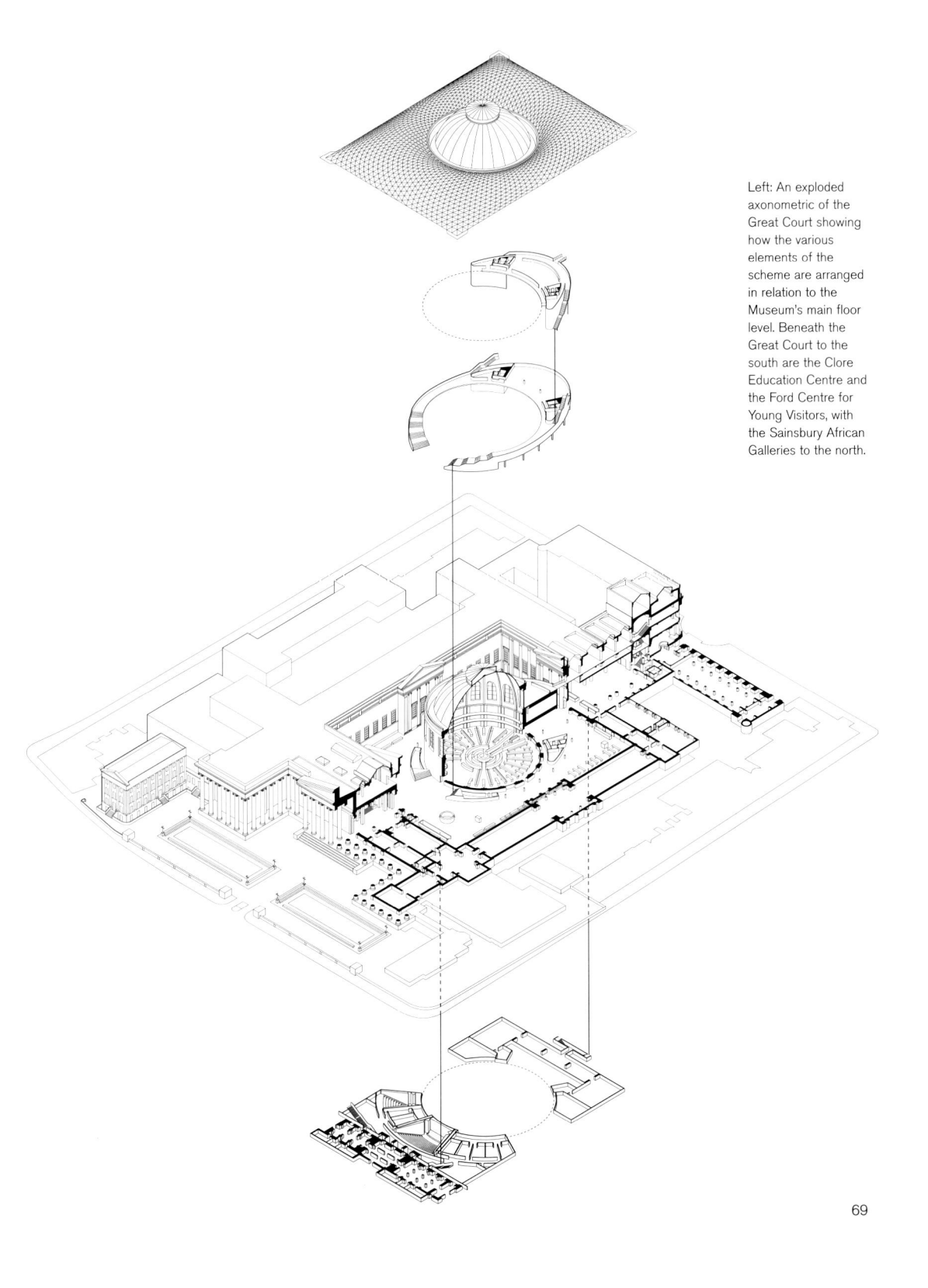

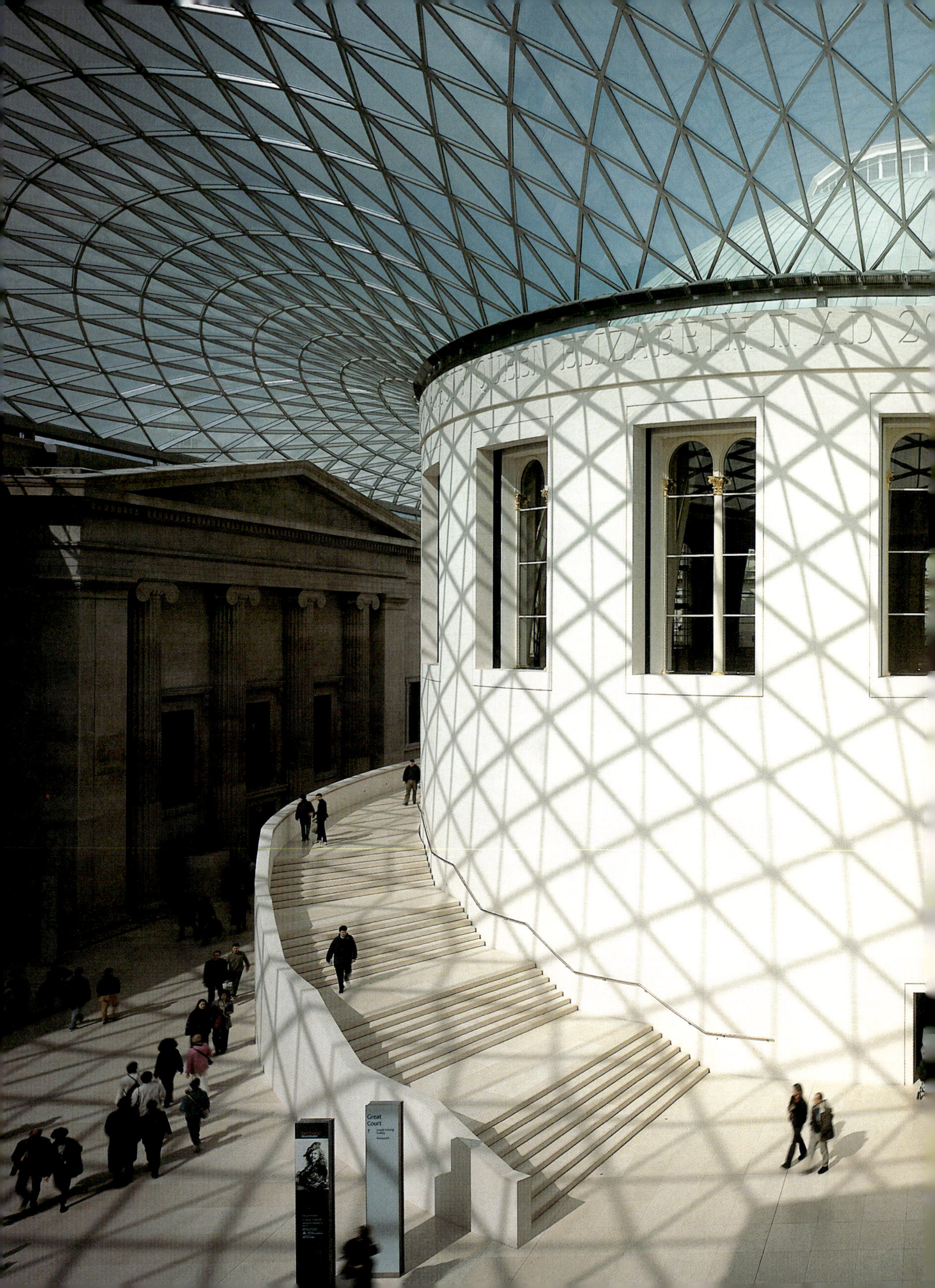
ELIZABETH II AD
Great Court

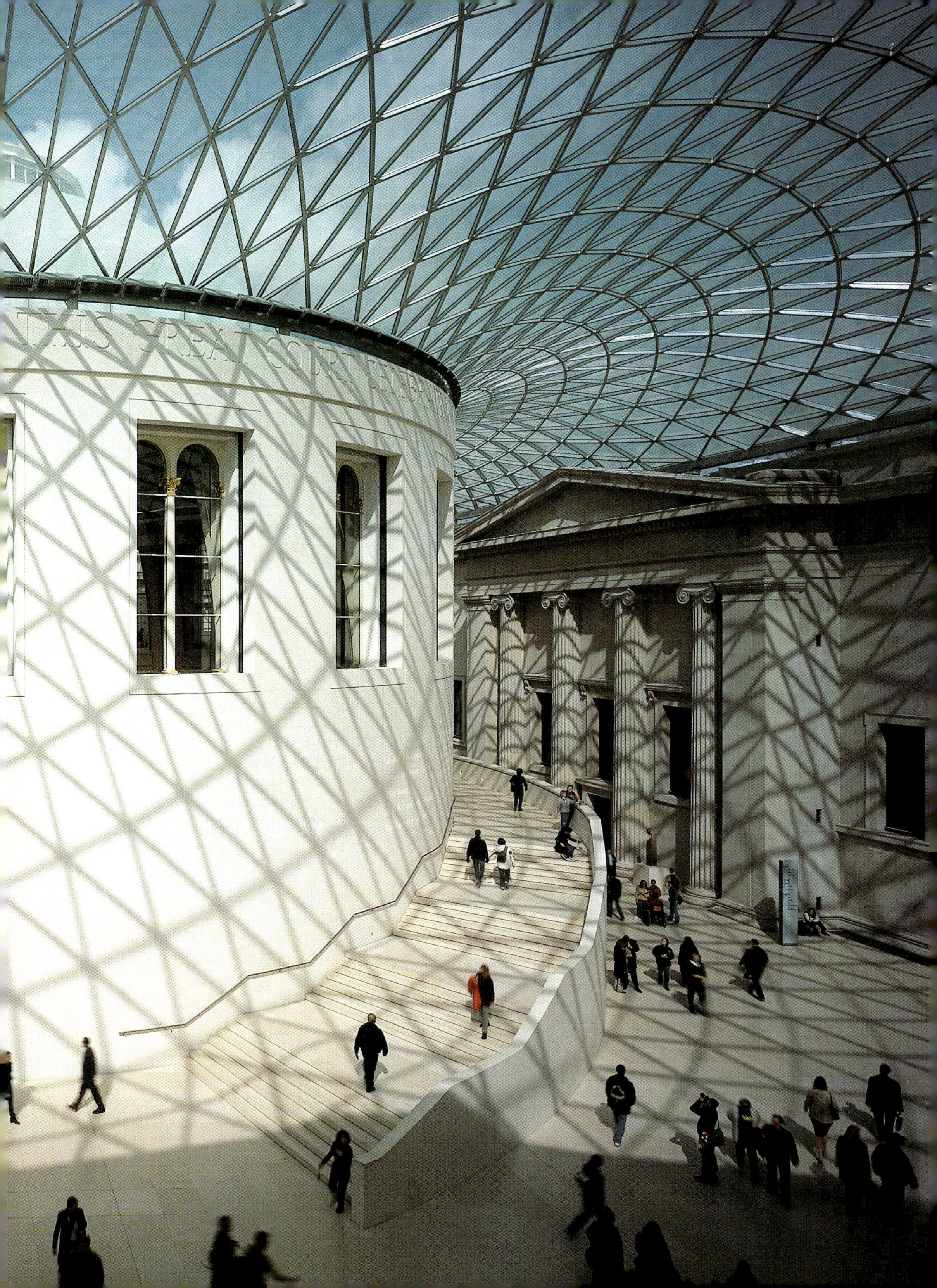
THIS GREAT COURT

The Museum Forecourt

Until its restoration, the forecourt had long been used as a car park for Museum and British Library staff. Apart from two walled rectangles of turf, the majority of the forecourt was covered in tarmac. Visitors to the Museum first passed through a sea of cars and then ranks of wooden benches. It was an inappropriate entrance to one of the world's great museums. Now, Robert Smirke's original geometry has been restored and seating integrated into new stone enclosures surrounding the reinstated turf. The cars have gone and the forecourt is paved in York stone or gravelled in the less trafficked areas. A major urban space has been returned to London.

Below: A plan of the forecourt; now restored it heralds the Great Court and forms a new public amenity in its own right.

Opposite: Robert Smirke's Ionic colonnade, completed in 1848, marks the main entrance, crowned by Richard Westmacott's pediment sculpture, installed in 1851.

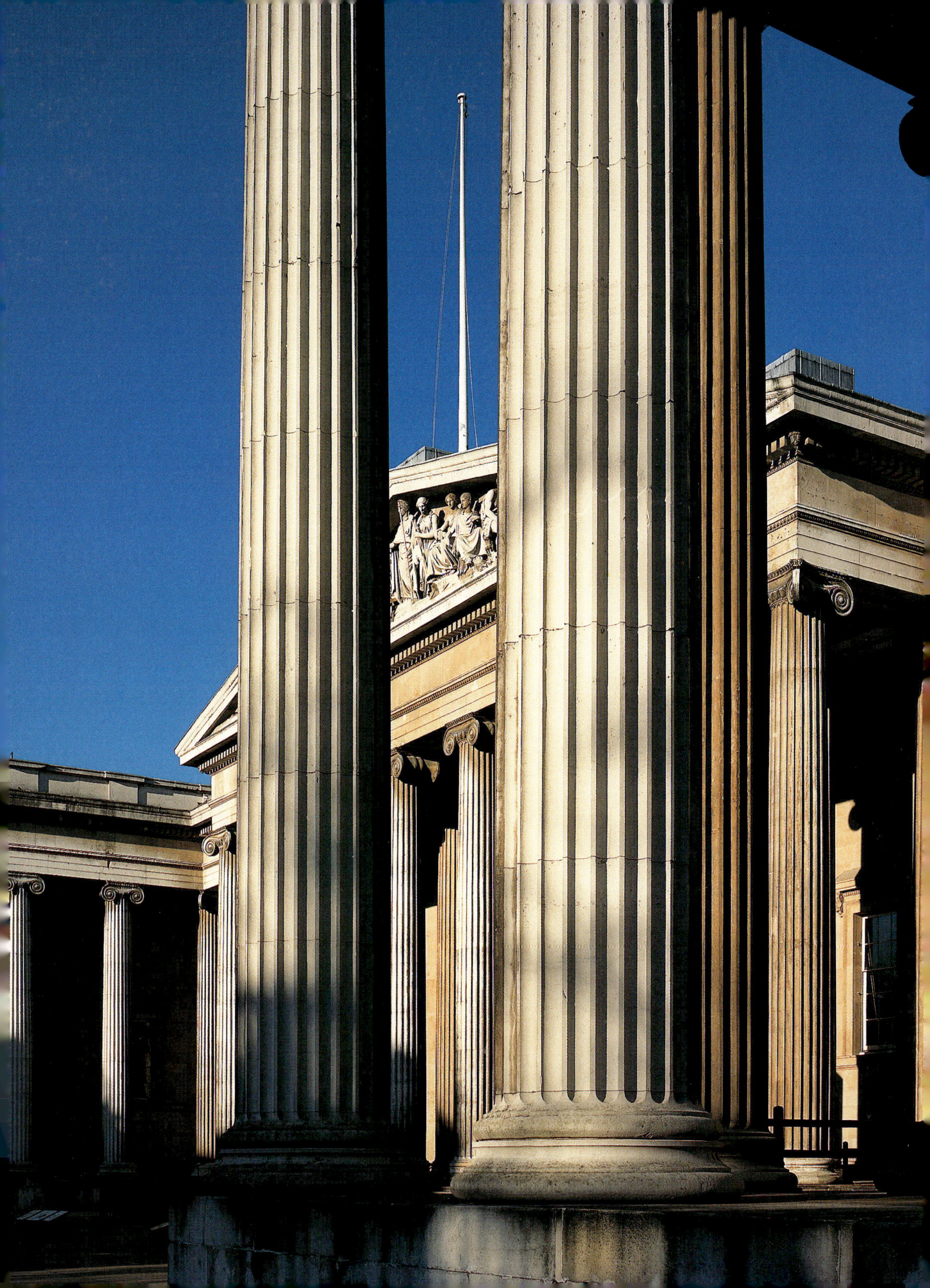

1995
Cluttered by cars and largely covered in tarmac, before its restoration the forecourt was a poor introduction to the Museum.

2000
Restored to its original formality, the forecourt offers an appropriate setting for the grandeur of the Museum and a much-improved amenity for visitors.

The Entrance Hall

Approaching up the grand flight of steps, visitors move through Robert Smirke's great portico into the entrance hall. This space was completed as part of the final phase of Smirke's masterplan for the Museum in 1846. In 1878 the hall was expanded by the addition of a third bay, which necessitated the demolition of the south portico. The entrance hall has now been restored to its original two-bay configuration with direct access into the Great Court via the rebuilt south portico.

The original decorative scheme within the entrance hall, devised by Sydney Smirke and executed by Messrs Collman and Davis, was historically important as the first major example in England of a design based upon contemporary archaeological excavations of Ancient Greek sites. As a result of detailed investigative work it has been possible to recreate this scheme faithfully using traditional painting and gilding techniques. The original carbon-arc light fittings have also been reinstated, using the manufacturer's working drawings, which were rediscovered in Germany.

Right: A detail of a contemporary catalogue illustration for the original carbon-arc light fittings designed for the Museum entrance hall and installed in 1879.

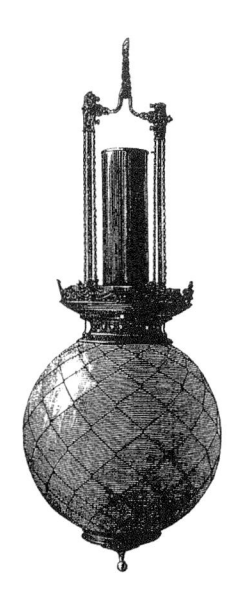

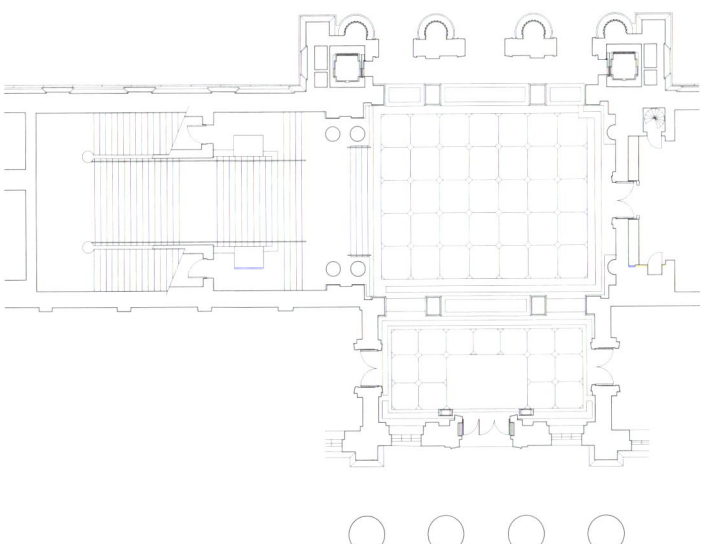

Above: The dramatic view from the entrance hall through the south portico and into the Great Court and the Reading Room beyond.

Left: A plan of the entrance hall. Upon entering the Museum visitors are now able to move directly through into the Great Court, thus greatly easing congestion.

77

1994
The entrance hall before restoration, looking towards the main staircase: it was a crowded and somewhat confusing space from which to embark upon a visit to the Museum.

2000
With its original decorative scheme restored the entrance hall forms a dazzling prelude to the Museum and the Great Court.

The Great Court

If the Museum can be thought of as a city, then the Great Court is its civic square. It is a major new social space for Londoners and has already become a popular rendezvous for those living and working in Bloomsbury. With two cafés on the main level and a restaurant above, it is possible to eat in the Great Court from early in the morning until late at night. Books and magazines can be bought at the new bookshop. It is a place to relax and contemplate the pleasures of the Museum or simply enjoy the 'street life' under the cover of the undulating glazed roof. A new floor level within the Great Court connects the galleries on the main floor and creates easy access to all parts of the Museum. By 2003, the 250th anniversary of the Museum's foundation, it is hoped that all Smirke's main level galleries will once again be linked by a continuous outer ring of circulation.

The ovoid structure that wraps around the drum of the Reading Room creates enclosures for much needed new accommodation, but its form has also been designed to aid movement around the Court. It swells and recedes in relation to the perimeter of the space, creating a dynamic interplay between the two. Two staircases form the southern end of the oval and lead to the Joseph Hotung Exhibition Gallery on the first floor. This is a flexible space designed to host small temporary exhibitions. The stairs continue to a new terrace restaurant, on the uppermost level, which affords excellent views of the Great Court and glimpses into the Reading Room.

From the restaurant level a bridge link takes visitors into the Museum's upper level galleries, which are mainly concentrated to the north. On the main level of the Court, the oval structure houses three new shops together with access to toilets and other facilities.

Opposite: A view of the stairs that wrap around the drum of the Reading Room and lead to the new temporary exhibitions gallery, on the first floor, and the restaurant above.

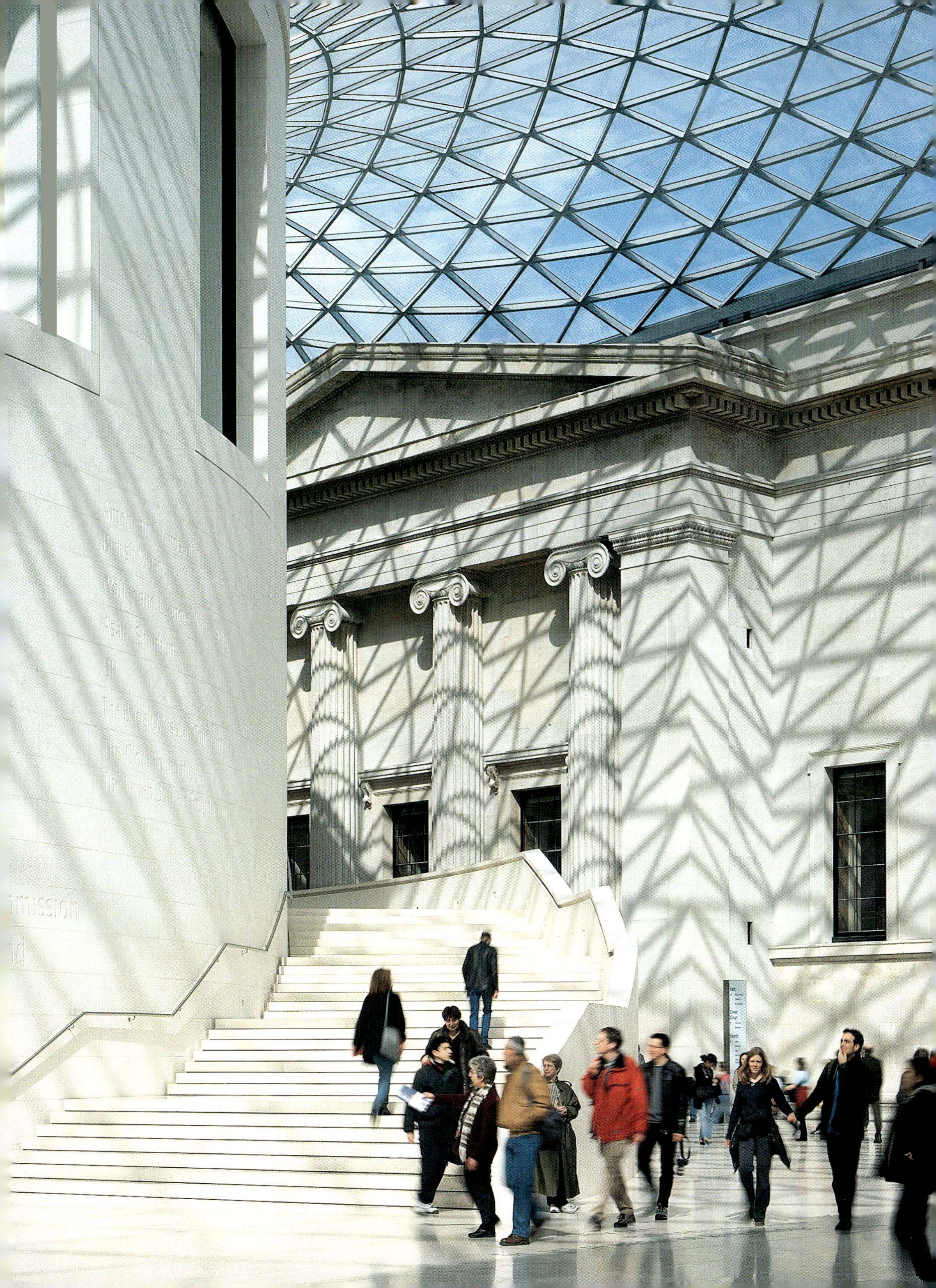
BP
The Clore Foundation and

1994
A view of the east portico and adjoining facade before the jumble of bookstacks and administrative buildings filling the Museum courtyard were removed.

2000
The corresponding view after the completion of the Great Court; the east portico is revealed, space, light and public access have been created.

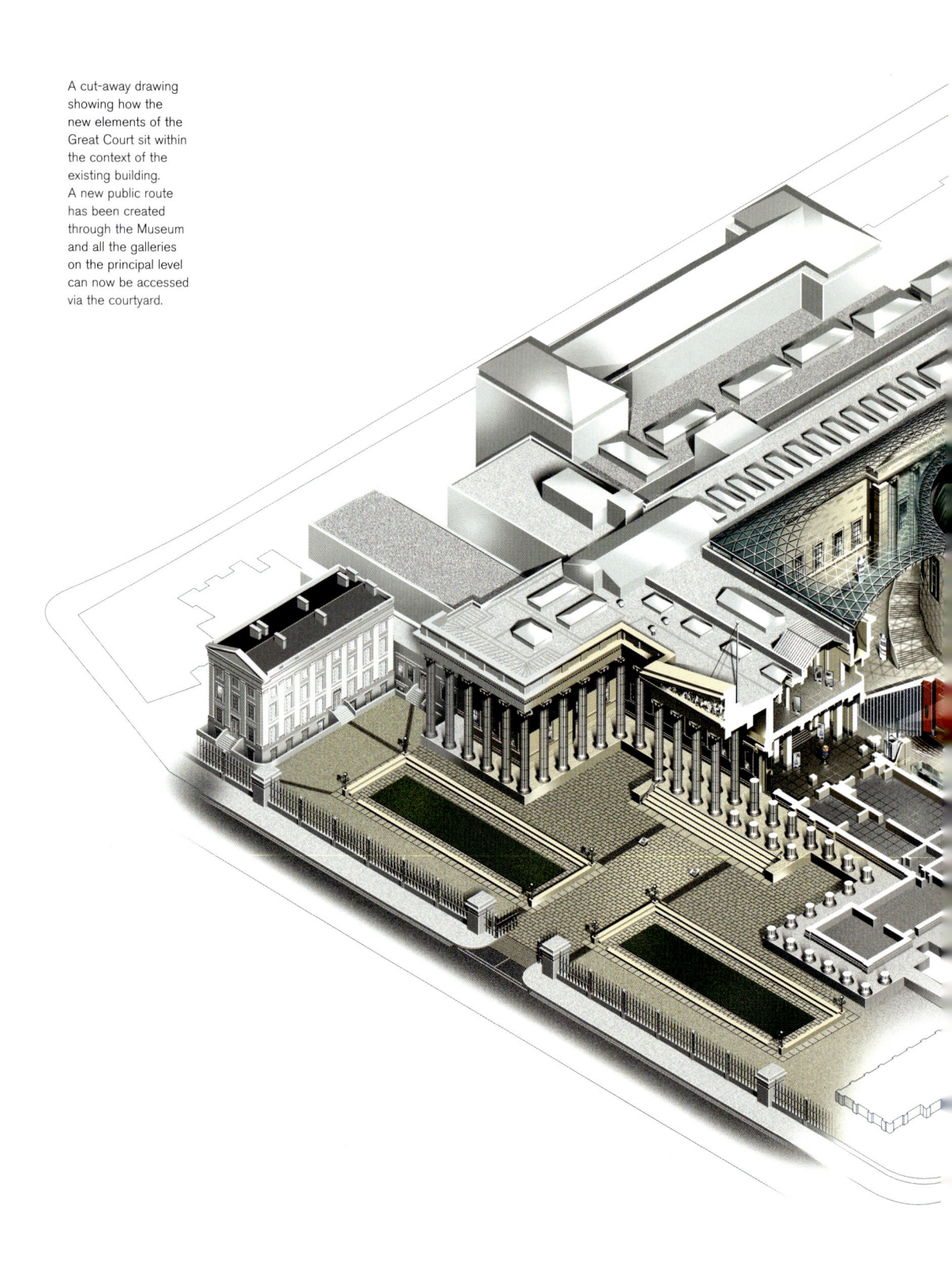

A cut-away drawing showing how the new elements of the Great Court sit within the context of the existing building. A new public route has been created through the Museum and all the galleries on the principal level can now be accessed via the courtyard.

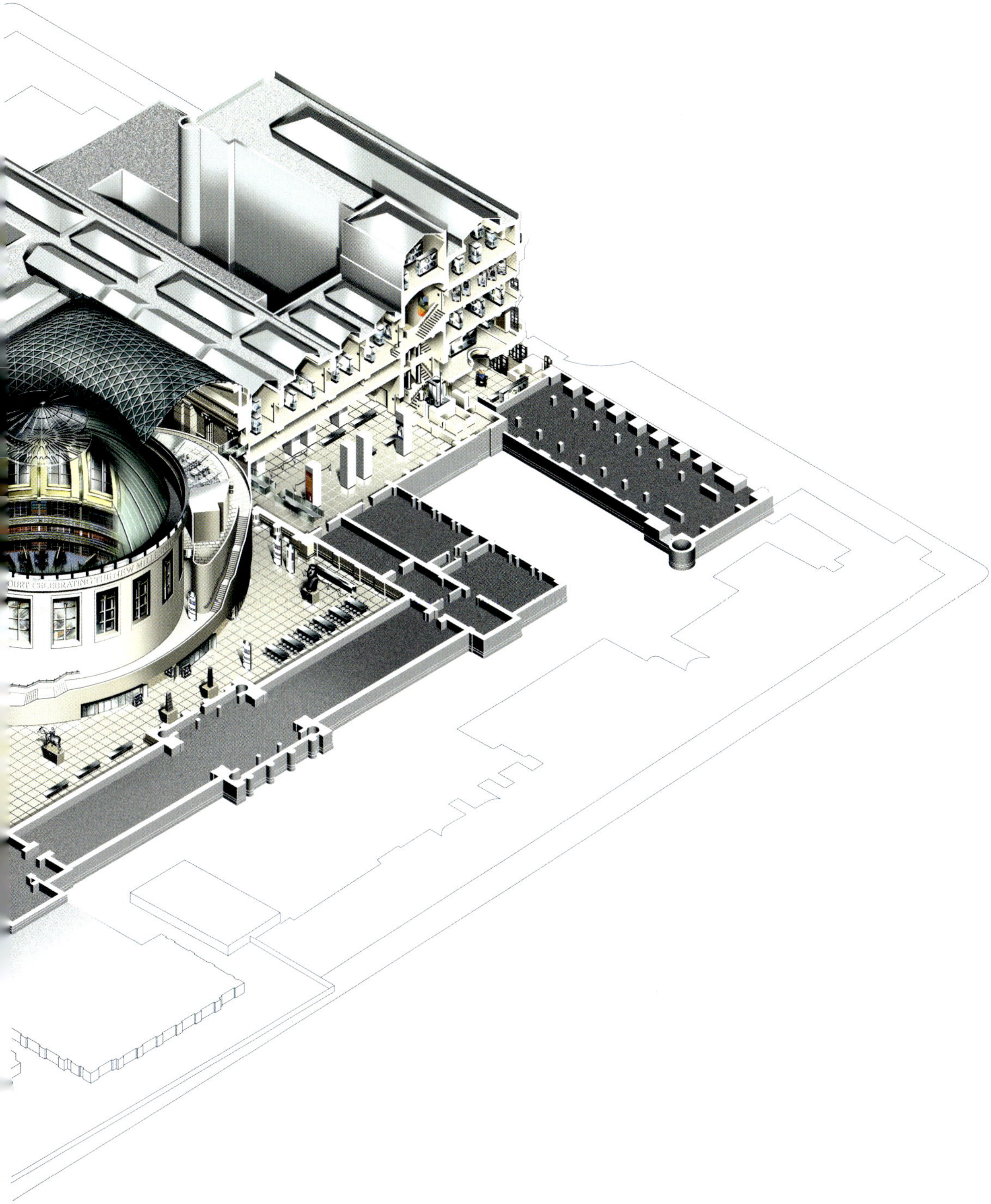

1994
A view of the north portico and the Reading Room before work on the Great Court began; bookstacks, offices and service ducts fill the courtyard.

2000

Right: An urban experience in microcosm: the light-flooded public space of the Great Court offers an architectural experience unlike any other in London.

Left: The success of the Great Court is evident in visitors' fascination with its various aspects and elements, and the familiarity and ease with which the public have claimed this space as their own.

89

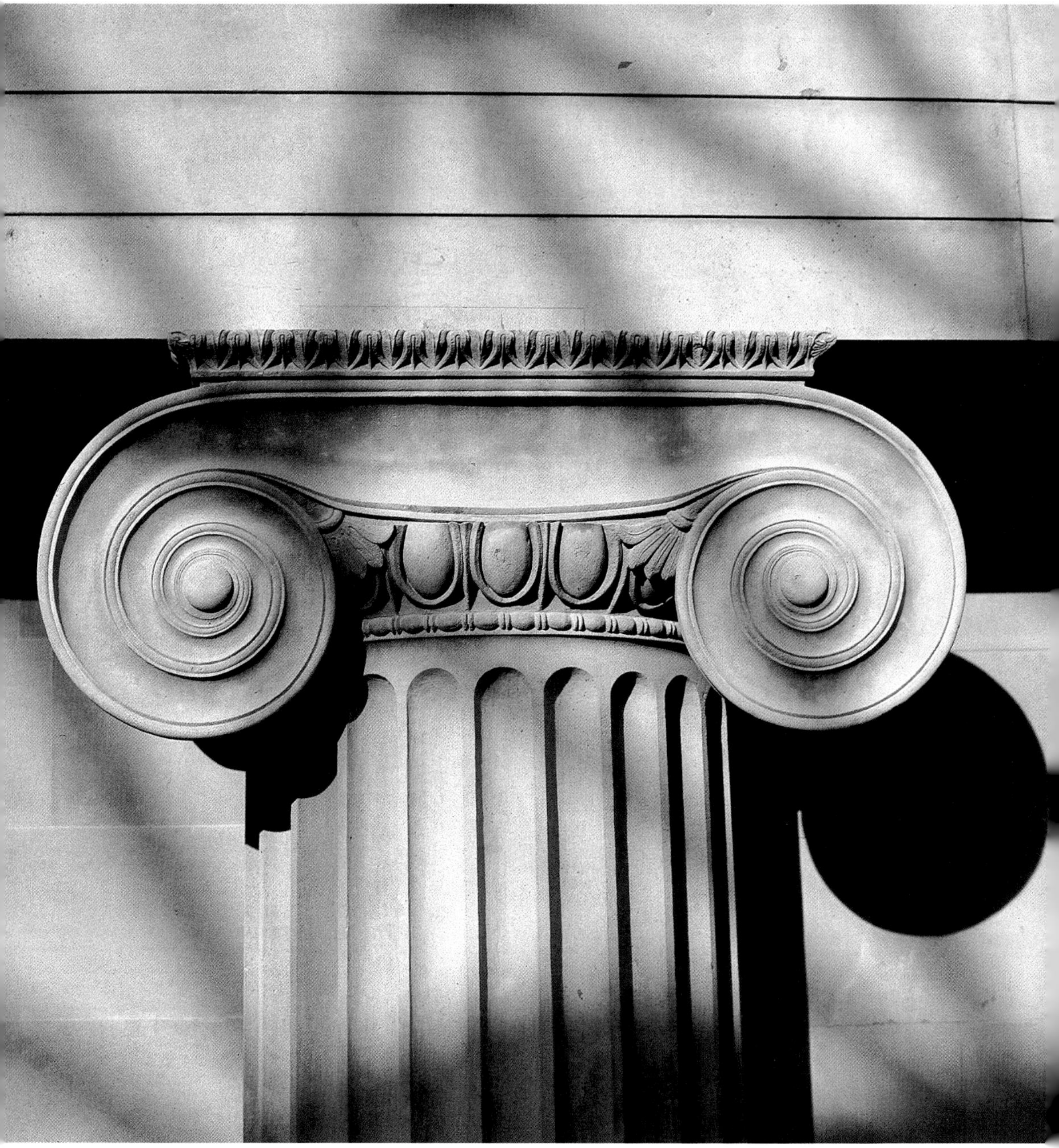

Left: Nineteenth-century engineering meets twentieth-century technology at the junction of the Reading Room drum and the steel and glass roof; the copper-clad Reading Room dome can be seen beyond.

Opposite: One of Robert Smirke's original stone capitals in the Great Court, its crisp carving now cleaned and restored.

Above: Occupying the upper level of the ovoid structure in the Great Court, the restaurant offers spectacular views of the activity below and the roof above.

Below: A bridge link connects the restaurant level with the existing Museum galleries to the north.

Above left: From the bridge visitors gain a new perspective on the surrounding facades.

Above right: A view of the restaurant, with its sheltering fabric awning.

Right: A new civic space: beneath the glass sky visitors can enjoy a range of amenities from early in the morning to late at night.

Opposite: The twin staircases embracing the drum of the Reading Room allow a variety of vantage points from which to view the Great Court.

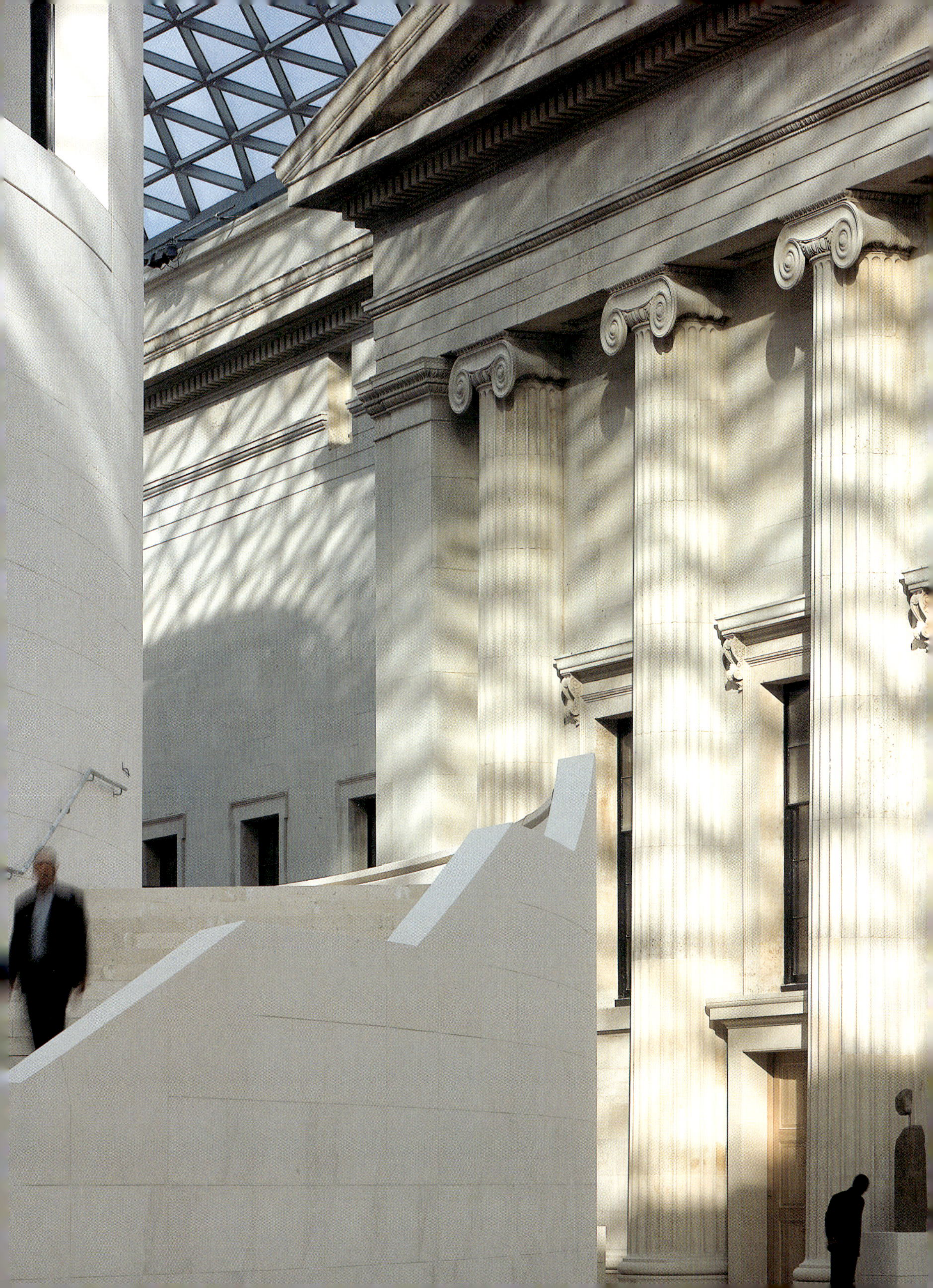

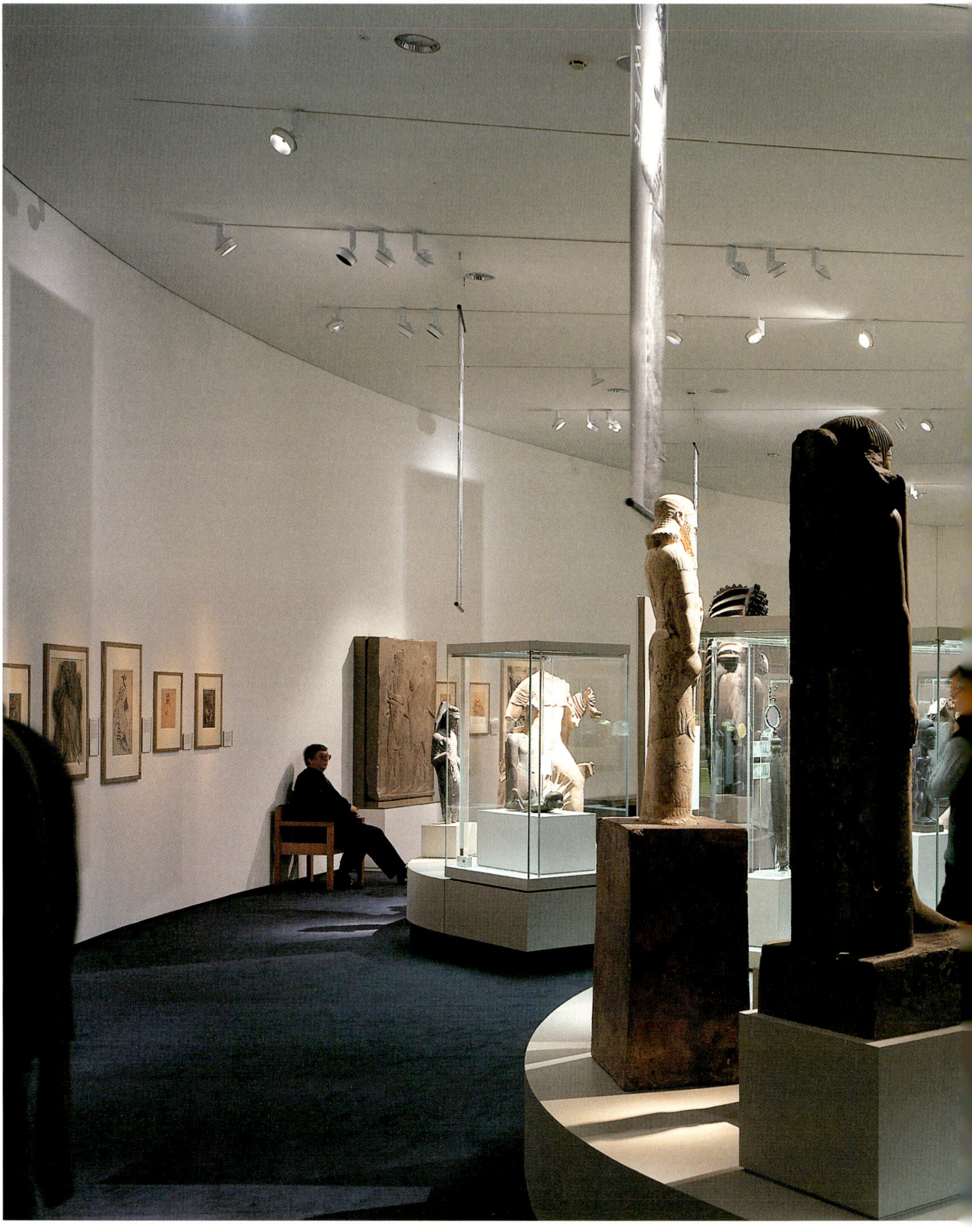

The first floor of the ovoid structure within the Great Court houses the Joseph Hotung Gallery. The creation of this new gallery has doubled the Museum's temporary exhibition space, thus ensuring that at least one themed exhibition is open to the public at any given time.

The Reading Room

Historically, only scholars and students engaged in academic research had access to the Reading Room. Now, as a new library of World Culture it is open to the general public for the first time and plays a central role as the main information centre within the Museum. It houses the Paul Hamlyn Library, a new 25,000-volume public reference library for the study of world civilisations within the Walter and Leonore Annenberg Centre. This is both literally and metaphorically the hub of the Museum. Here visitors can use the latest technology to access COMPASS, a database that allows a virtual tour of the Museum's collections or spend time in quiet private study.

The Reading Room was originally intended to be viewed only from the inside: its only external facade comprised utilitarian brickwork from the window level upwards. Below window level bookstack buildings were attached directly to the structural frame. Now that the exterior of the drum has been revealed it has been clad in limestone from the Cabra quarries, north of Granada in Spain. The use of limestone for the Reading Room unites the free-standing structures with the Great Court's original facades and the new floor, the solid, earthbound elements providing a foil to the lightness of the steel and glass roof.

Within the Reading Room the radial layout of tables has been retained and the furniture and fittings restored. The original fresh-air ventilation system – in which grilles in the legs of the tables are served from a 'spider' of air ducts below the floor – has been reopened, while stale air extract and smoke venting is through the new service void formed around the rotunda.

Opposite: Restored to its former glory, the Reading Room is open to the general public for the first time in its history.

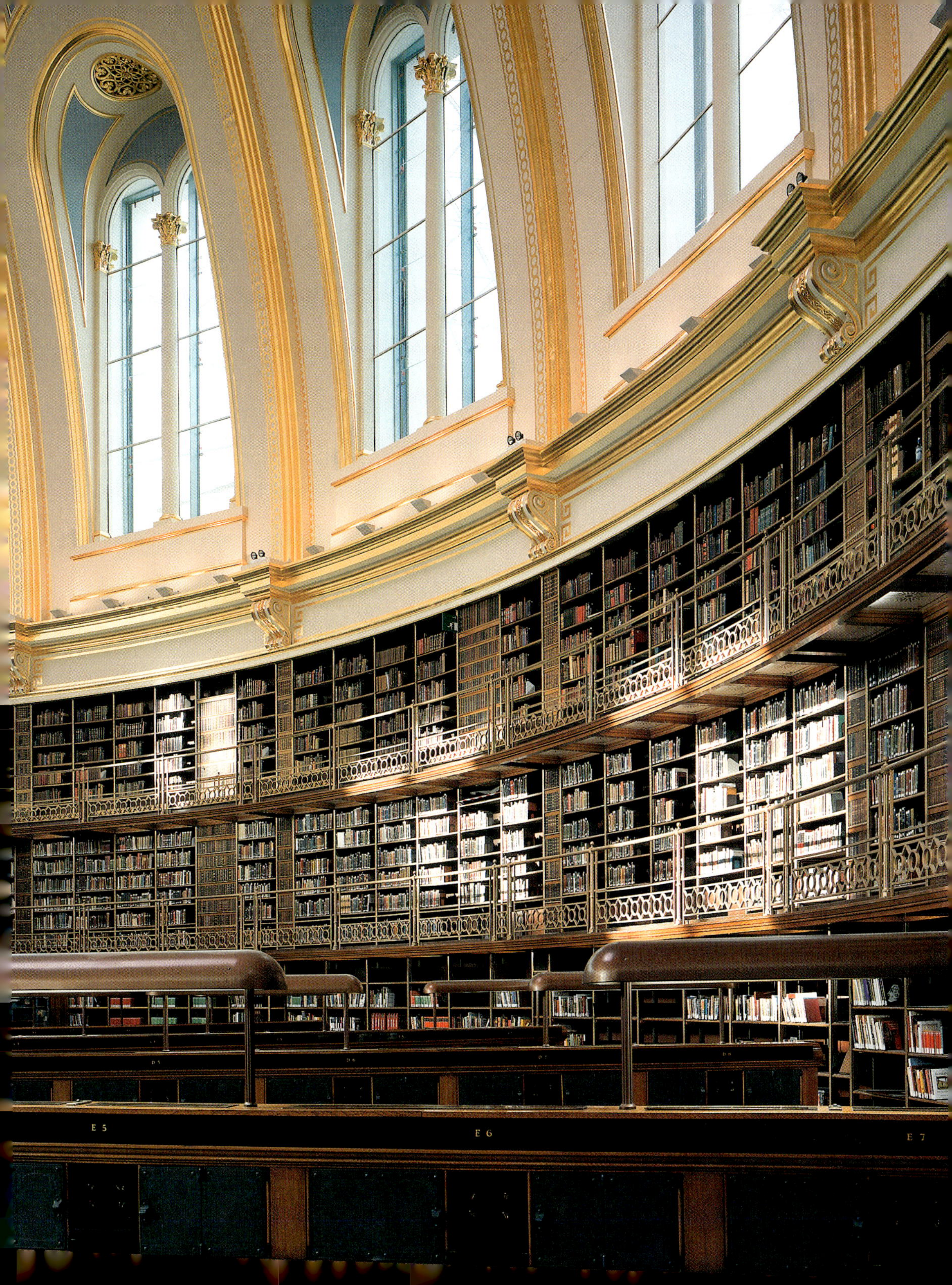
E 5
E 6
E 7

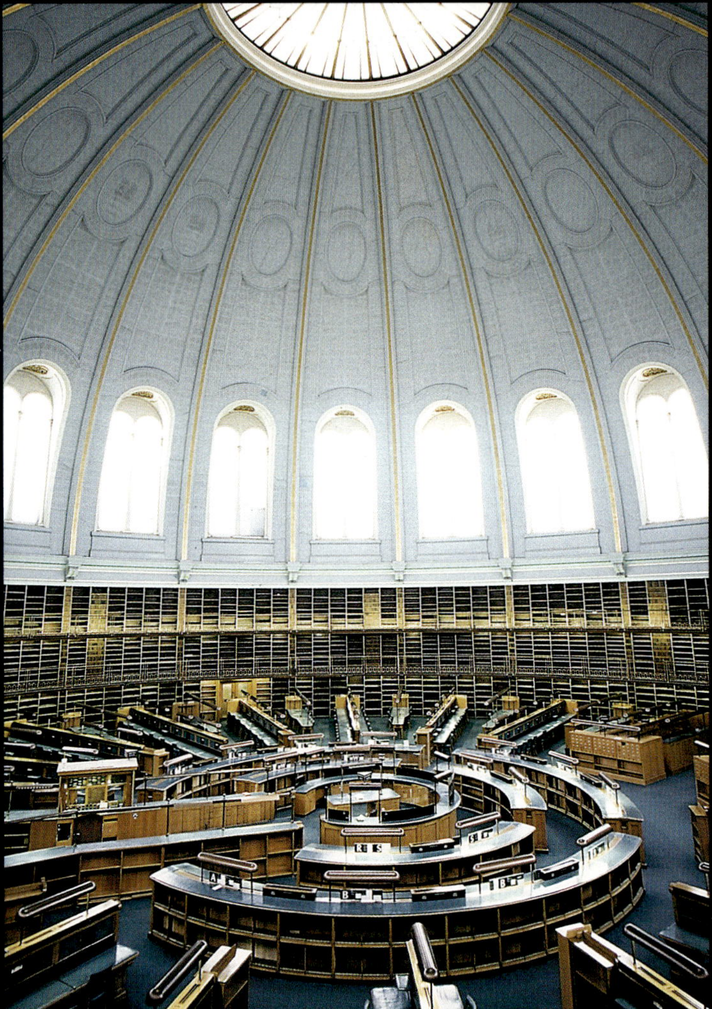

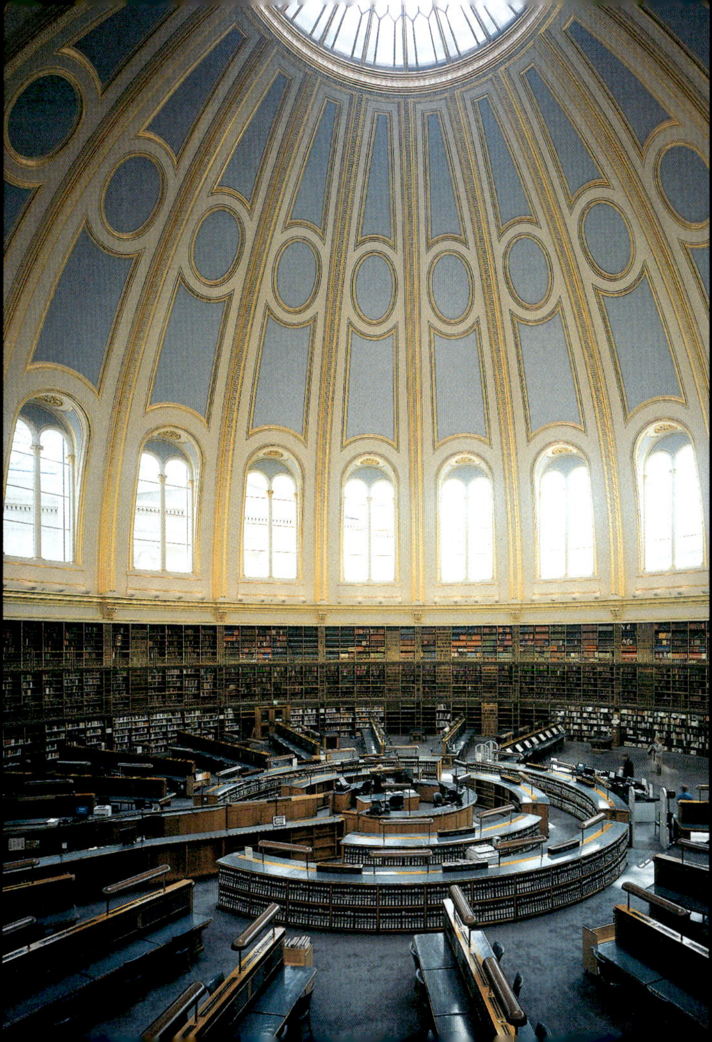

The interior of the dome, which is 43 metres (140 feet) in diameter – some 9 metres (29 feet) greater than that of St Paul's and only slightly less than that of the Pantheon in Rome – has been restored to its original splendour. The dome's papier mâché lining (a patented form of wood-pulp board) has been carefully restored. To avoid future cracking caused by the movement of the cast-iron frame the lining was repaired using a material similar to surgical bandage, which allows the structure to flex in response to changes in temperature without affecting the painted surface. As a result, when many people get their first glimpse of this imposing room they will see it as Sydney Smirke originally intended, with the azure, cream and gold decorative scheme he devised in 1857.

Above: A temporary platform rising 29 metres (94 feet) into the Reading Room lantern was erected to enable restoration of the dome.

Opposite: As the scaffolding was removed, the impact of the newly restored colour scheme was revealed, April 2000.

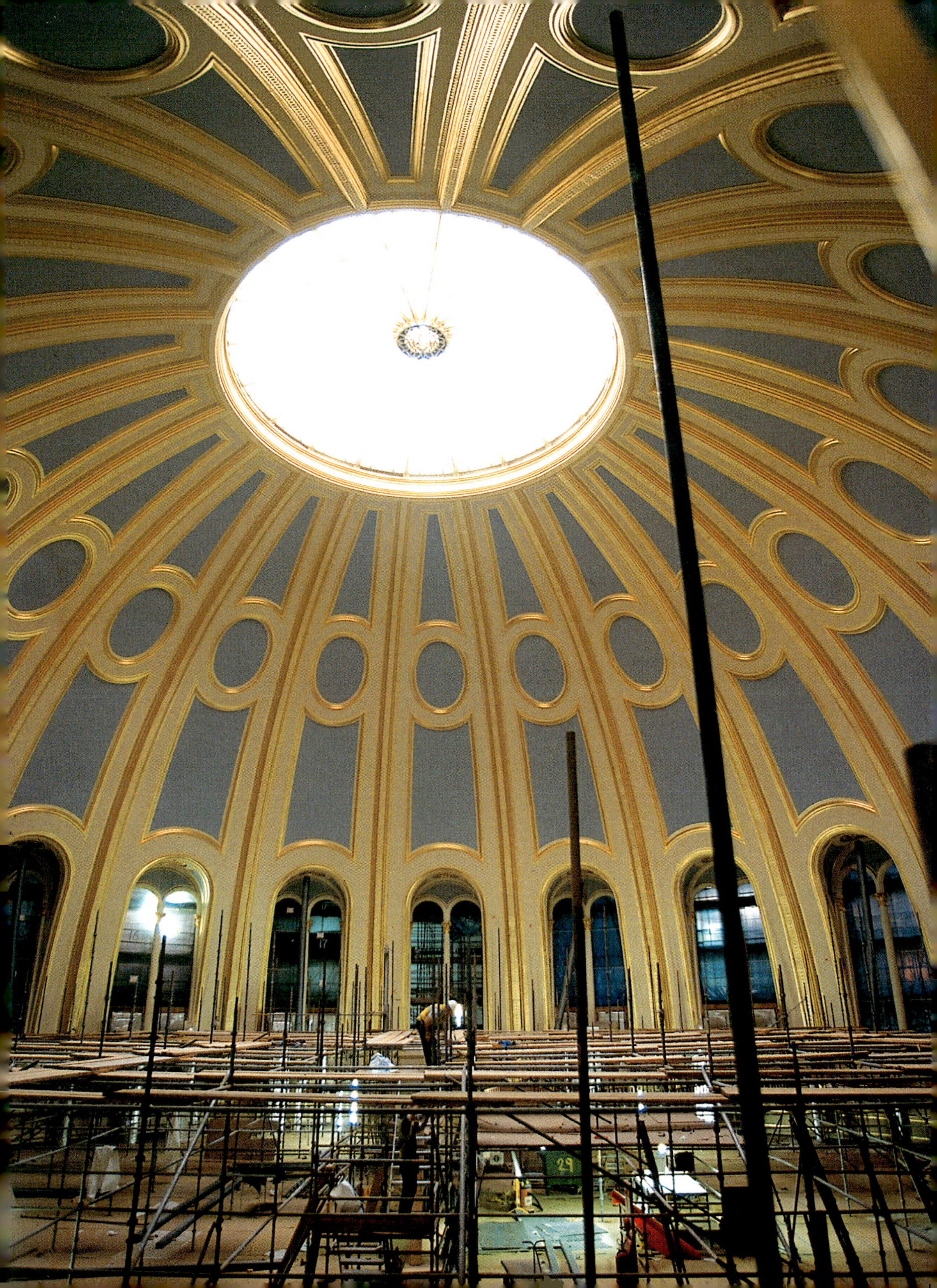

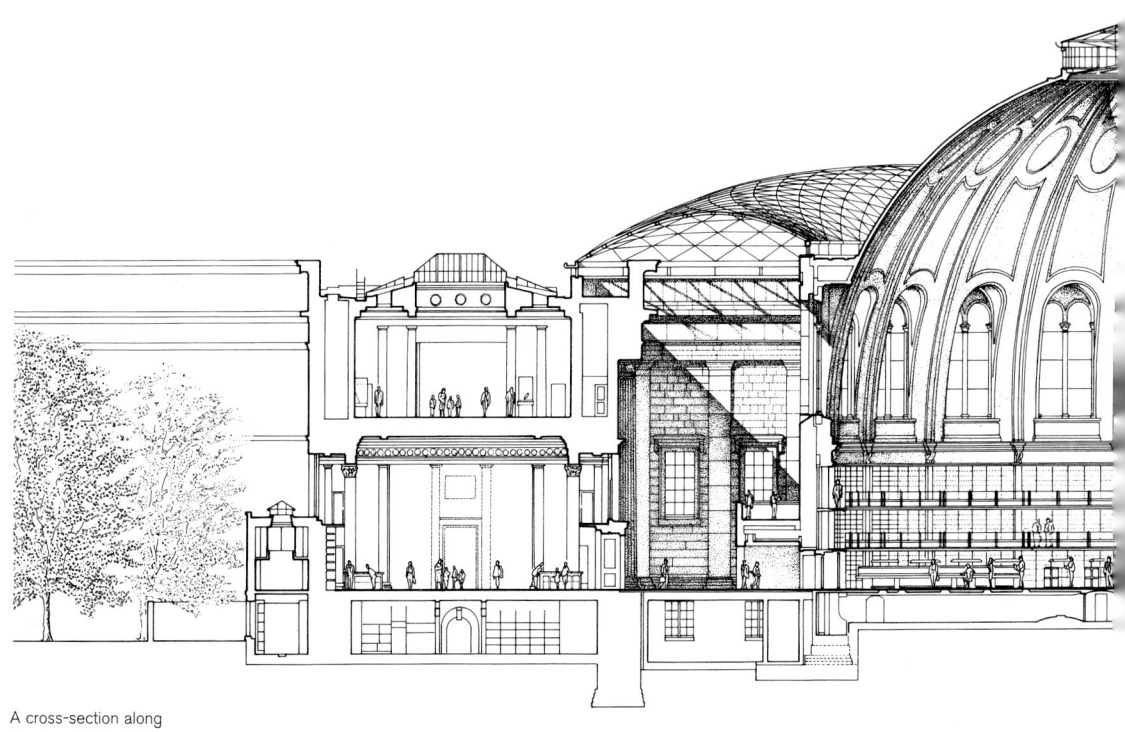

A cross-section along the building's east-west axis reveals the heroic scale of the Reading Room when compared with the surrounding galleries and highlights the extent of the newly created public space within the Museum.

104

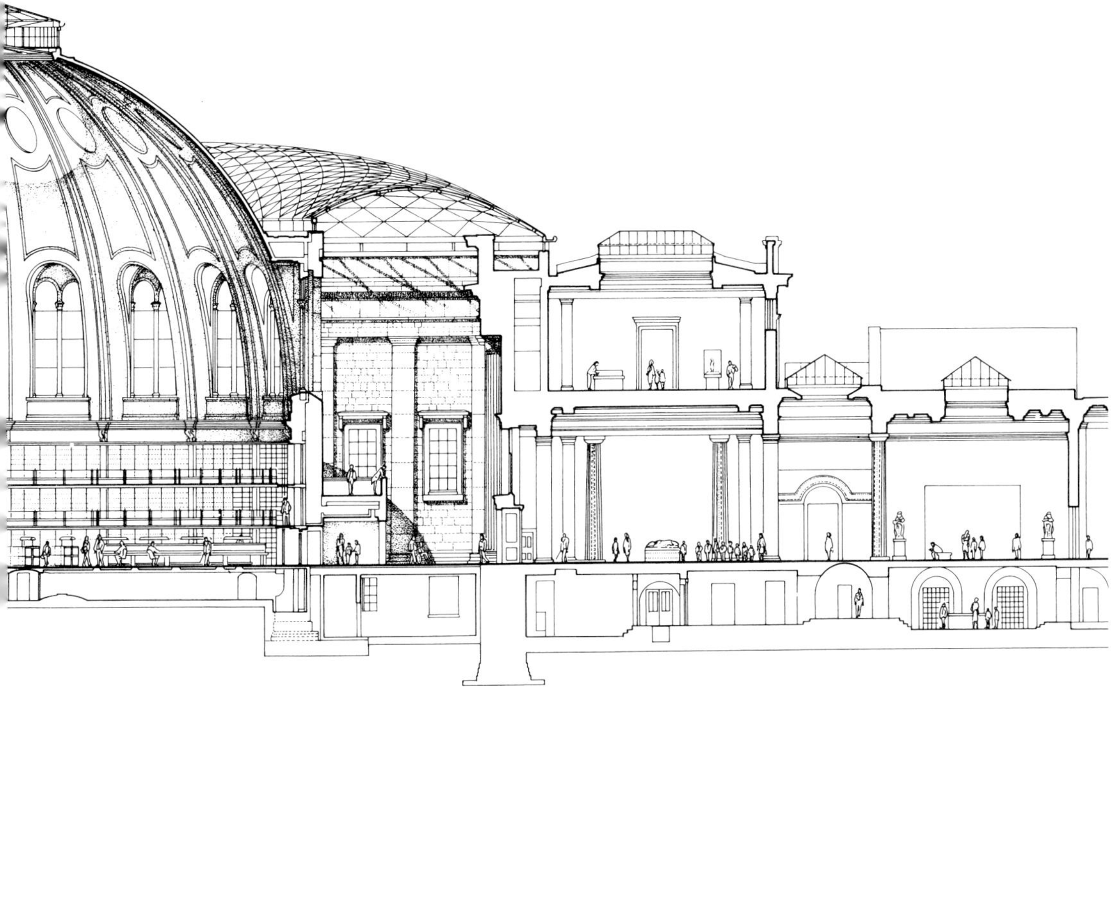

The Clore Education Centre

To the south of the Reading Room, at a new level excavated 9 metres (29 feet) below the Great Court, is the Clore Education Centre. It contains two auditoria and five seminar rooms, all linked by a grand curving foyer. The larger auditorium can seat an audience of 320, the smaller 150 people. These new facilities will meet the needs of the Museum's expanding education programme and allow it to stage major conferences and seminars on an international scale.

Above Left: The sweeping curve of the Clore Education Centre foyer leads to the auditoria and seminar rooms.

Above right: The larger of the two auditoria, which has greatly enhanced the British Museum's conference facilities.

Left: Twin staircases provide access and bring light to the lower levels of the Great Court.

The Ford Centre for Young Visitors

The Education Centre is reached via two staircases in the Great Court, which bring light and views to the lower areas. Halfway down these stairs is the entrance to the Ford Centre for Young Visitors. It is situated at the level of the original courtyard garden in the Victorian brick vaults beneath the main entrance. The vaults have been carefully restored and fitted-out with purpose-designed furniture. The Centre provides facilities for the 1,500 school children that visit the Museum daily.

Below: The spacious, brick-vaulted Ford Centre for Young Visitors.

The Sainsbury African Galleries

In 1970, due to the lack of space in Bloomsbury, the British Museum's African and other ethnographic collections were moved to Burlington Gardens to become the Museum of Mankind. Now returned to the Museum, Ethnography will be located in the north wing vacated by the British Library. The Sainsbury African Galleries are located below the Great Court to the north of the Reading Room. Five inter-linked rooms create over 900 square metres (9,700 square feet) of new gallery space. These rooms have been designed as simple, flexible enclosures to allow the display of the collection, which will be changed on a regular basis. The African galleries will be linked to new galleries for American, Asian and Pacific cultures thus offering the possibility of appreciating the British Museum's fine ethnographic holdings in the context of the other great works in the collection.

Above and opposite: Located in the lower levels of the Great Court, the Sainsbury Galleries provide space for the display of the Museum's African collection, which is among the finest in the world.

Complementing the Sainsbury Galleries, the Wellcome Gallery will form the focal point for Ethnography in the Museum. This space, adjacent to the Great Court, on the main Museum level has been created from what was once the North Library, the second major reading room of the British Library. From here, access can be gained to other ethnographical galleries to the east and west as well as the African Galleries beneath. It is an important part of the north-south public route through the Museum which will only be fully realised when the north staircase is altered to make an axial approach.

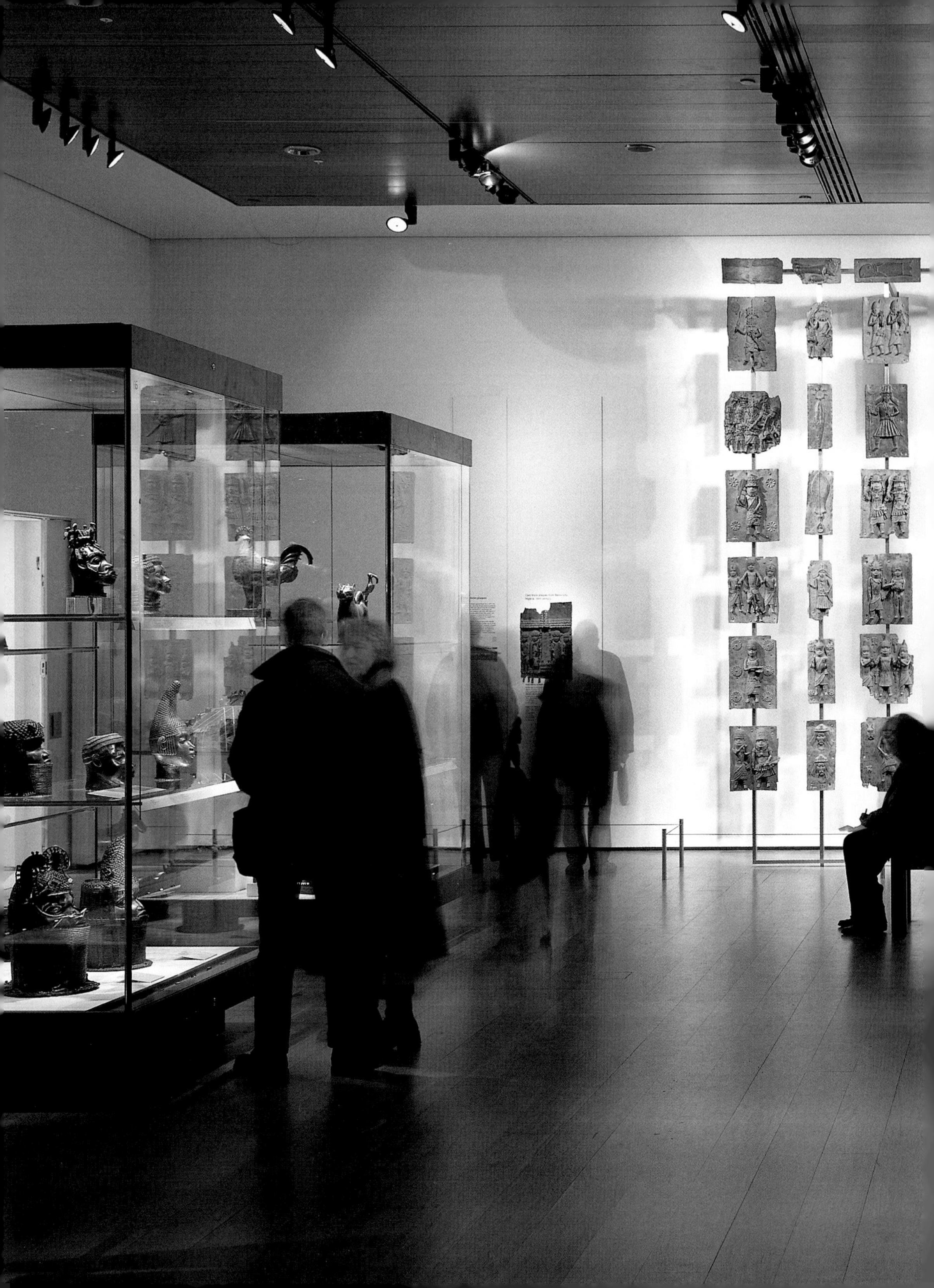

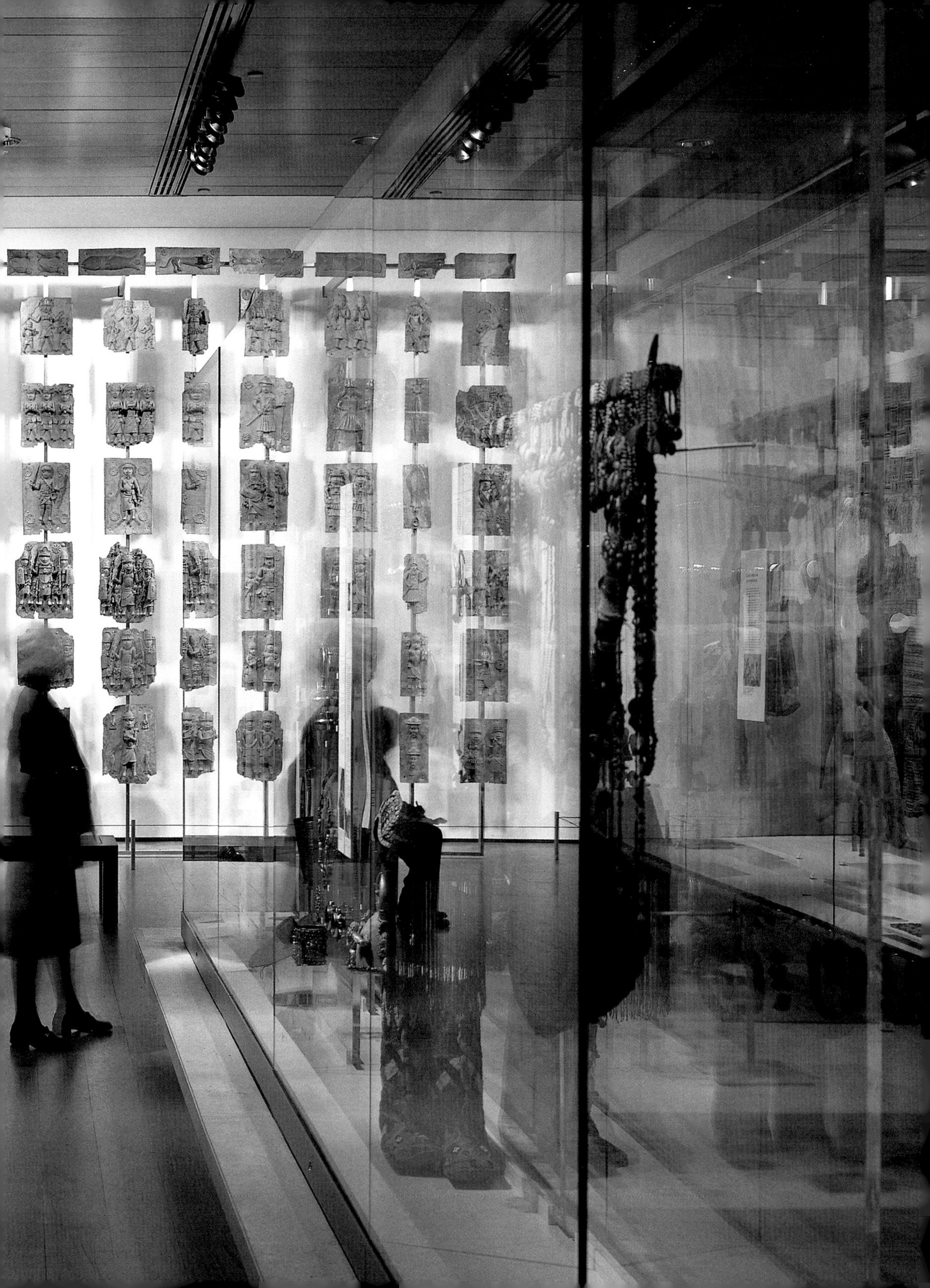

Facts and Figures

General

Cost of project:
  £100 million
Gross project area:
  22,600 square metres
  (243,265 square feet)

Foster and Partners
scheme announced:
  24 July 1994
Construction Begun:
  2 March 1998
Official Opening:
  6 December 2000

The Great Court

Area of inner courtyard:
  7,100 square metres
  (76,400 square feet)
Weight of concrete used to build
the foundations and new principal
floor of the courtyard:
  16,000 tonnes
Volume of material removed
in the demolition process:
  20,000 cubic metres
  (26,180 cubic yards) –
  equivalent to twice that of
  the Museum's Egyptian
  Sculpture Gallery or 12
  Olympic swimming pools.
Weight of stone quarried
to build the south portico:
  1,500 tonnes
Largest piece of stone:
  7 tonnes
Area of restored courtyard
facade stonework:
  6,000 square metres
  (64,585 square feet)

The Reading Room

Reading Room ground floor area:
  1,350 square metres (14,530
  square feet) – approximately
  21% of the ground area of
  the courtyard
Height from the floor to the
apex of the dome:
  33 metres (107 feet)
Diameter of dome:
  43 metres (140 feet) –
  exceeding the dome of St Paul's
  Cathedral, which measures 34
  metres (111 feet)
Diameter of lantern:
  12 metres (39 feet)
Temporary scaffolding deck:
  entire room spanned at a height
  of 7 metres (23 feet), with a
  central tower rising 29 metres
  (94 feet) into the lantern

The Roof
Overall dimensions:
    96 metres by 72 metres
    (312 by 234 feet)
Overall area:
    7,100 square metres
    (76,400 square feet)
Maximum distance spanned:
    40 metres (130 feet)
Minimum distance spanned:
    14 metres (46 feet)
Highest point above floor level:
    26 metres (85 feet)
Diameter of structural ring around
the Reading Room drum:
    44 metres (143 feet)
Weight of steel:
    478 tonnes
Number of individual steel members:
    5,162
Number of structural nodes:
    1,826, each of which is unique
Weight of glass:
    315 tonnes
Number of individual glass panels:
    3,312

Above: The Reading Room ablaze with light during a reception for Museum staff, October 2000.

Overleaf: Zulu dancers from the Adzido dance troupe welcome the Queen at the ceremony to mark the official opening of the Great Court, 6 December 2000.

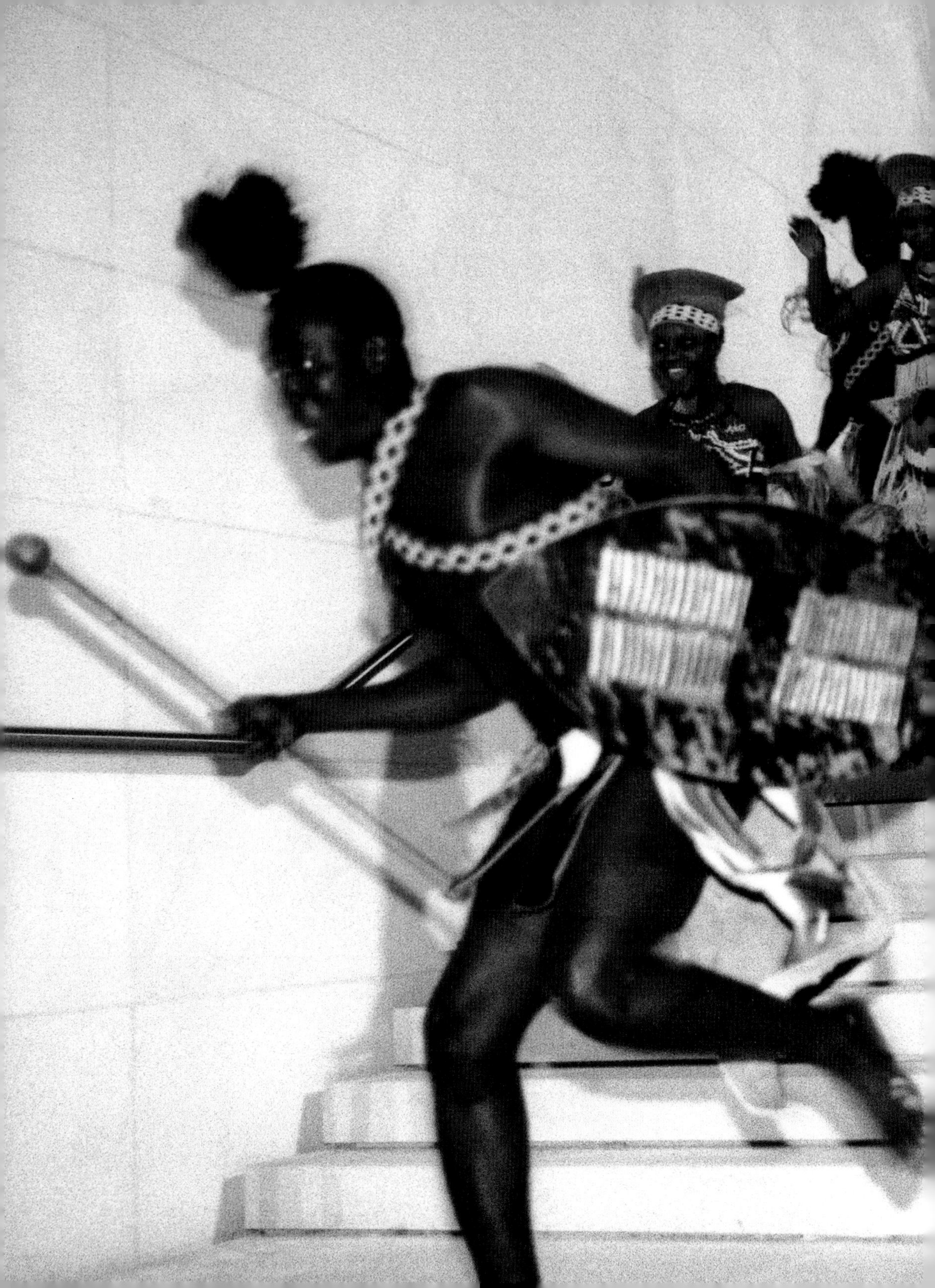

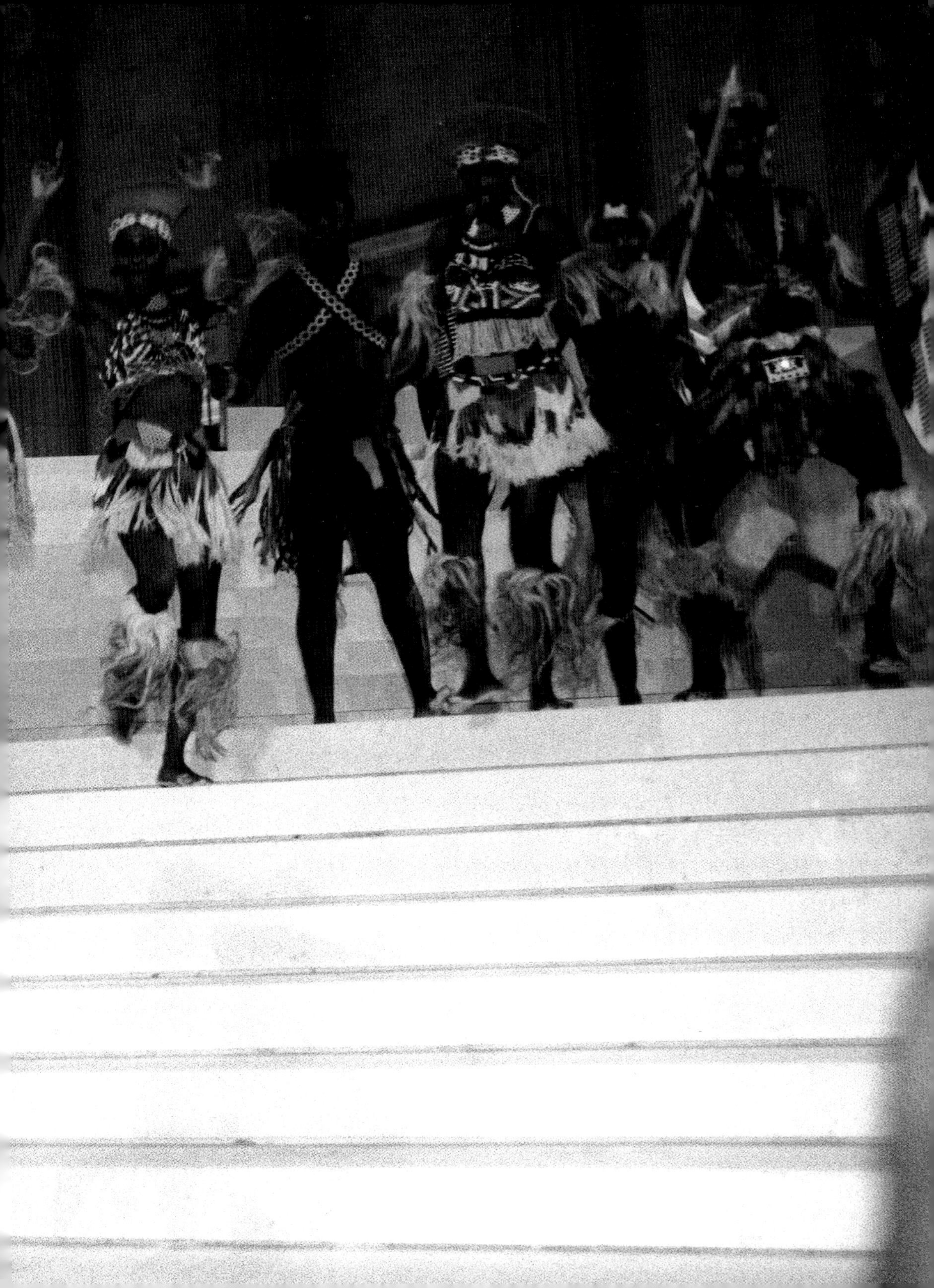

Team Credits

Foster and Partners
Norman Foster
Spencer de Grey
Giles Robinson
Michael Jones
Julia Abell
William Castagna
Mark Costello
Daniel Goldberg
Nesa Marojevic
Peter Matcham
Filo Russo
Paul Simms
Peter Vandendries
Oliver Wong
Diane Ziegler

Norman Foster graduated from Manchester University School of Architecture and City Planning in 1961 and won a Fellowship to Yale University where he gained a Masters Degree in architecture. In 1963 he co-founded Team 4 and in 1967 he established Foster Associates, now known as Foster and Partners. The practice has its main studio in London, with project offices worldwide.

He was awarded the RIBA Royal Gold Medal for Architecture in 1983, the Gold Medal of the French Academy of Architecture in 1991 and the American Institute of Architects Gold Medal in 1994. Also in 1994, he was appointed Officer of the Order of Arts and Letters by the Ministry of Culture in France. In 1999 he became the 21st Pritzker Architecture Prize Laureate. He was granted a knighthood in the Queen's Birthday Honours of 1990, appointed by the Queen to the Order of Merit in 1997 and in 1999 was honoured with a life peerage, taking the title Lord Foster of Thames Bank.

He has lectured throughout the world and taught architecture in the United States and the United Kingdom. He has been vice president of the Architectural Association in London, a council member of the Royal College of Art, a member of the Board of Education and visiting examiner for the Royal Institute of British Architects and is a trustee of the Architecture Foundation of London.

Spencer de Grey studied architecture at Cambridge University. As a student he worked on a competition entry for a new city at Espoo in Finland that was highly placed in a large entry. On leaving Cambridge in 1969, he worked for the London Borough of Merton on one of the first middle schools in the country.

He joined Foster Associates in 1973, continuing his work in education on the Palmerston Special School in Liverpool. In 1979 he set up Foster Associates' office in Hong Kong to build the Hongkong and Shanghai Bank. In 1981 he returned to London to become the director in charge of Stansted Airport, which was completed in 1991. During this period, he also worked on the BBC Radio Centre and was responsible for the Sackler Galleries at the Royal Academy of Arts in London.

Since becoming a partner in 1991, he has overseen a wide range of projects, including Cambridge Law Faculty, the Commerzbank Headquarters in Frankfurt, the Great Court at the British Museum, the Great Glasshouse at the National Botanic Garden of Wales, the World Squares for All Masterplan for London and Boston Museum of Fine Arts Masterplan.

He is a trustee for the Royal Botanical Gardens in Kew, a governor of the Building Centre Trust and is on the board of London First. He was made a CBE in the Queen's Birthday Honours of 1997.

Client and Consultants

Client
 Trustees of the British Museum
Acoustic Engineering
 Sandy Brown Associates
Audio Visual
 Mark Johnson Consultants
Catering
 Digby Trout Restaurants
 Tricon Foodservice Consultants
Construction Manager
 MACE Ltd
Façade Engineering
 Emmer Pfenninger & Partners
Fire Engineering
 FEDRA
Gallery Fitout
 British Museum Design Dept
 with George Sexton
Historic Building Advisor
 Giles Quarme Associates
 Caroe and Partners
 Ian Bristow
Lighting Design
 Claude Engle
Mechanical & Electrical
 Buro Happold Engineers
Planning Supervisor
 Buro Happold
Quantity Surveyors
 Northcroft Nicholson
 Davis Langdon & Everest
Shop Fitout
 Carte Blanche
Signage
 Baumann & Baumann
Structural Engineers
 Buro Happold

Suppliers and Subcontractors

Architectural Metalwork
 Glazzard (Dudley) Ltd (General)
Audio Visual
 RSL Presentation Systems Plc
Auditoria Seating
 Poltrona Frau
Auditorium Grilles and Linings
 Sherlock Interiors Ltd
Builders' Work 1
 Aldersbrook Construction Ltd
Catering Fit Out
 Martek Contracts Ltd
Commissioning Management
& Technical Authoring
 Dome Building Services Project
 Management Ltd
Controls and BMS
 CSI Projects Ltd
Dry Lining, Plastering
& Suspended Ceilings
 ASTEC Projects Ltd
Electrical Services
 N G Bailey & Company Ltd
Existing Gates and Railings
 Capricorn Architectural
 Ironwork Ltd
External Works
 McNicholas Plc
Final Clean
 Connaught Cleaning Services Ltd
Fit Out
 Alandale Construction Ltd
Forecourt Archaeology
 Pre-Construct Archaeology
Front Hall Access Scaffold
 Fourways Plant Ltd
General Decorations
 Johns of Nottingham Ltd
Integrated Furniture
 Tecno (GB) Ltd
Lift Installations
 Associated Lift Services Ltd

Mechanical Services
 Sulzer Infra (UK) Ltd
Multi Service Gang
 Alandale Construction Ltd
Reading Room Refurbishment
 E J Tracey Ltd
Reading Room Ceiling
 Hare & Humphreys
Reception Desks
and Information Totems
 Marzorati Ronchetti
Repairs to Reading Room Roof
 Alexio Metal Roofing Company Ltd
Roof Steelwork and Glazing
 Waagner-Biro Binder
Servery Counters
 Design Counters Ltd
Signage Lettering
 Bull Signs Ltd
Specialist Light Fixtures
 Erco Lighting Ltd
Sprinklers
 Matthew Hall Ltd
Soft Floor Finishes
 Rees Floor Ltd
Stone Cladding
 Grants of Shoreditch Ltd
Stone Façade Restoration
 St Blaise Ltd
 Easton Masonry
Temporary Electrics
 Electrical Mechanical
 Services UK Ltd
Toilet Fit Out
 Ardmac Performance
 Contracting Ltd
Windows
 Littlehampton Welding Ltd

Further Reading

Select bibliography

Anderson, Robert, The Great Court and the British Museum, London, 2000

Anderson, Robert, The British Museum, London, 1997

Caygill, Marjorie, Building the British Museum, London, 1999

Caygill, Marjorie, The British Museum companion guide, London, 1998

Caygill, Marjorie, The Story of the British Museum, London, 1992

Cowtan, Robert, Memories of the British Museum, London, 1872

Crook, J Mordaunt, The British Museum, London, 1972

De Beer, G R, Sir Hans Sloane and the British Museum, London, 1953

Edwards, Edward, Lives of the Founders, and Notes of some Chief Benefactors and Organizisers of the British Museum, London, 1870

Esdaile, Arundell, The British Museum Library, London, 1946

Fothergill, B, Sir William Hamilton, London, 1969

Harris, P R, A History of the British Museum Library 1753-1973, London, 1998

Harris, P R, The Reading Room, London, 1986

Jenkins, Ian, Archaeologists and Aesthetes; in the Sculpture Galleries of the British Museum 1800-1939, London, 1992

Kenyon, F, The Buildings of the British Museum, London, 1914

MacGregor, Arthur, Sir Hans Sloane: collector, scientist, antiquary, founding father of the British Museum, London, 1994

Miller, Edward, That Noble Cabinet: a history of the British Museum, London, 1973

Miller, Edward, A Brief History of the British Museum, London, 1970

Paintin, Elaine M, The King's Library, London, 1989

St Clair W, Lord Elgin and the Marbles, Oxford, 1983

Shelley, Henry Charles, The British Museum: its history and treasures, London, 1911

Wilson, David M, The Collections of the British Museum, London, 1991

Wilson, David M, The British Museum: purpose and politics, London, 1989

Wilson, David M, The British Museum and its Public, London, 1982

Periodicals and Journals

Crook, J Mordaunt, 'Sir Robert Smirke: a Regency Architect in London,' Journal of the London Society, no. 381, March 1968

De Beer, G, 'Sir Hans Sloane and the British Museum', British Museum Quarterly, 18, 1953, pp. 2-4

Dunlop, I, 'The First Home of the British Museum', Country Life 110, 1951, pp. 812-14

Glancey, Jonathan, 'The British Museum Extension', Architectural Review, 169, January 1981, pp. 46-52

Hart, Sara, 'A Brilliant Shell Game at the British Museum', Architectural Record, 189, March 2001, pp. 149-54

Kendrick, Thomas, 'The British Museum, 1753-1953', Country Life, 113, 1953, pp. 1876-78

Pevsner, Nikolaus, 'The British Museum, 1753-1953', Architectural Review, 113, 1953 pp. 179-82

Powell, Kenneth, 'Holding Court', Architect's Journal, 212, December 2000, pp. 24-31

Sanders, Andrew, 'The British Museum', AA Files, 6, May 1984, pp. 50-7

Sudjic, Deyan, 'The Monument in the Museum', Domus, 834, February 2001, pp. 36-53

Credits

Picture Credits
l = left, m = middle, r = right,
t = top, b = bottom.
Thanks are due to the following for permission to reproduce copyright photographs and drawings:

Arcaid/Richard Bryant: 55(t), 73, 101
Birds Portchmouth Russum: 88-9 (fold-out), 104-5
The British Museum, London: 14, 16
R. Buckminster Fuller Papers, California: 10(l)
Richard Davies: 38, 39, 40, 41(t), 43(t)
Norman Foster: 6, 8-9, 11(b)
Ti Foster: 64, 90, 91
Foster and Partners: 7(r), 35, 41(b), 42, 43(bl-r), 44, 45(ml-r, b), 54-5(b), 56, 72, 74, 76, 77(b), 82, 86
Yukio Futagawa: 117(l)
Galleria Nazionale delle Marche, Urbino, Bridgeman Art Library: 11(t)
Gregory Gibbon: 84-5
John Hewitt: 30, 31, 34, 65, 69
Hulton Archive: 15, 23, 24, 25, 26
The Illustrated London News Picture Library: 20, 21
Ben Johnson: 12-13
Mary Evans Picture Library: 10(r), 17, 22
National Monuments Record © The Warburg Institute: 27
Tim Soar: 93(bl), 88(tl, tr, br), 89(tl, br)
View/Dennis Gilbert: 7(l), 33, 95, 99
Visum/Rudi Meisel: 117(r)
Nigel Young: 4, 18-19, 28-9, 36-7, 45(t), 47, 48, 51, 52, 53, 58, 59, 60, 61, 62, 63, 66-7, 70-1, 75, 77(t), 78, 79, 81, 83, 87, 88(l), 89(bl), 92, 93(t, br), 94, 96-7, 100, 102, 103, 106, 107, 108, 109, 110-1, 113, 114-5, 116

Book Credits
Editing
    David Jenkins, Gerard Forde,
    Sophie Carter, Philippa Baker
Picture Research
    Kate Stirling, Stephan Potchatek,
    Katy Harris, Sophie Hartley
Design
    Thomas Manss & Company
    Thomas Manss, Laia Roses
    Lisa Sjukur
Book Production
    Turner Libros, Madrid